THE HUMAN BODY
How It Works

# Human Development

# THE HUMAN BODY
## How It Works

## THE HUMAN BODY
### How It Works

# Human Development

Ted Zerucha

INTRODUCTION BY

## Denton A. Cooley, M.D.
President and Surgeon-in-Chief
of the Texas Heart Institute
Clinical Professor of Surgery at the
University of Texas Medical School, Houston, Texas

## CHELSEA HOUSE
### P U B L I S H E R S
An imprint of Infobase Publishing

Chelsea House
An imprint of Infobase Publishing
132 West 31st Street
New York NY 10001

**Library of Congress Cataloging-in-Publication Data**

Zerucha, Ted, 1967-
  Human development / Ted Zerucha.
    p. cm. — (The human body: how it works)
  Includes bibliographical references and index.
  ISBN 978-1-60413-371-4 (hardcover)
  1. Embryology, Human—Juvenile literature. I. Title. II. Series.

  QM601.Z47 2009
  612.6'4—dc22                                    2008052356

Chelsea House books are available at special discounts when purchased in bulk
quantities for businesses, associations, institutions, or sales promotions. Please call
our Special Sales Department in New York at (212) 967-8800 or (800) 322-8755.

You can find Chelsea House on the World Wide Web at
http://www.chelseahouse.com

Series design by Erika Arroyo, Erik Lindstrom
Cover design by Takeshi Takahashi

Printed in the United States of America

Bang EJB 10 9 8 7 6 5 4 3 2 1

This book is printed on acid-free paper.

All links and Web addresses were checked and verified to be correct at the time of
publication. Because of the dynamic nature of the Web, some addresses and links may
have changed since publication and may no longer be valid.

# Contents

# Introduction

THE HUMAN BODY IS AN INCREDIBLY COMPLEX AND amazing structure. At best, it is a source of strength, beauty, and wonder. We can compare the healthy body to a well-designed machine whose parts work smoothly together. We can also compare it to a symphony orchestra in which each instrument has a different part to play. When all of the musicians play together, they produce beautiful music.

From a purely physical standpoint, our bodies are made mainly of water. We are also made of many minerals, including calcium, phosphorous, potassium, sulfur, sodium, chlorine, magnesium, and iron. In order of size, the elements of the body are organized into cells, tissues, and organs. Related organs are combined into systems, including the musculo-skeletal, cardiovascular, nervous, respiratory, gastrointestinal, endocrine, and reproductive systems.

Our cells and tissues are constantly wearing out and being replaced without our even knowing it. In fact, much of the time, we take the body for granted. When it is working properly, we tend to ignore it. Although the heart beats about 100,000 times per day and we breathe more than 10 million times per year, we do not normally think about these things. When something goes wrong, however, our bodies tell us through pain and other symptoms. In fact, pain is a very effective alarm system that lets us know the body needs attention. If the pain does not go away, we may need to see a doctor. Even without medical help, the body has an amazing ability to heal itself. If we cut ourselves, the blood-clotting system works to seal the cut right away, and the immune defense system sends out special blood cells that are pro-grammed to heal the area.

During the past 50 years, doctors have gained the ability to repair or replace almost every part of the body. In my own field of cardiovascular surgery, we are able to open the heart and repair its valves, arteries, chambers, and connections. In many cases, these repairs can be done through a tiny "keyhole" incision that speeds up patient recovery and leaves hardly any scar. If the entire heart is diseased, we can replace it altogether, either with a donor heart or with a mechanical device. In the future, the use of mechanical hearts will probably be common in patients who would otherwise die of heart disease.

Until the mid-twentieth century, infections and contagious diseases related to viruses and bacteria were the most common causes of death. Even a simple scratch could become infected and lead to death from "blood poisoning." After penicillin and other antibiotics became available in the 1930s and 1940s, doctors were able to treat blood poisoning, tuberculosis, pneumonia, and many other bacterial diseases. Also, the introduction of modern vaccines allowed us to prevent childhood illnesses, smallpox, polio, flu, and other contagions that used to kill or cripple thousands.

Today, plagues such as the "Spanish flu" epidemic of 1918–19, which killed 20 to 40 million people worldwide, are unknown except in history books. Now that these diseases can be avoided, people are living long enough to have long-term (chronic) conditions such as cancer, heart failure, diabetes, and arthritis. Because chronic diseases tend to involve many organ systems or even the whole body, they cannot always be cured with surgery. These days, researchers are doing a lot of work at the cellular level, trying to find the underlying causes of chronic illnesses. Scientists recently finished mapping the human genome, which is a set of coded "instructions" programmed into our cells. Each cell contains 3 billion "letters" of this code. By showing how the body is made, the human genome will help researchers prevent and treat disease at its source, within the cells themselves.

The body's long-term health depends on many factors, called risk factors. Some risk factors, including our age, sex, and family history of certain diseases, are beyond our control. Other important risk factors include our lifestyle, behavior, and environment. Our modern lifestyle offers many advantages but is not always good for our bodies. In western Europe and the United States, we tend to be stressed, overweight, and out of shape. Many of us have unhealthy habits such as smoking cigarettes, abusing alcohol, or using drugs. Our air, water, and food often contain hazardous chemicals and industrial waste products. Fortunately, we can do something about most of these risk factors. At any age, the most important things we can do for our bodies are to eat right, exercise regularly, get enough sleep, and refuse to smoke, overuse alcohol, or use addictive drugs. We can also help clean up our environment. These simple steps will lower our chances of getting cancer, heart disease, or other serious disorders.

These days, thanks to the Internet and other forms of media coverage, people are more aware of health-related matters. The average person knows more about the human body than ever before. Patients want to understand their medical conditions and treatment options. They want to play a more active role, along with their doctors, in making medical decisions and in taking care of their own health.

I encourage you to learn as much as you can about your body and to treat your body well. These things may not seem too important to you now, while you are young, but the habits and behaviors that you practice today will affect your physical well-being for the rest of your life. The present book series, THE HUMAN BODY: HOW IT WORKS, is an excellent introduction to human biology and anatomy. I hope that it will awaken within you a lifelong interest in these subjects.

Denton A. Cooley, M.D.
*President and Surgeon-in-Chief*
*of the Texas Heart Institute*
*Clinical Professor of Surgery at the*
*University of Texas Medical School, Houston, Texas*

# 1

# What Is Development?

DEVELOPMENT IS THE PROCESS BY WHICH A SINGLE CELL becomes a multicellular organism. In humans, this process takes approximately 264 days, or 9 months. During that time, cells divide many times to produce the millions of cells found in the human body. This collection of cells undergoes a vast number of events at the molecular and cellular levels to produce a complete human body. As a result of a process called **differentiation**, the cells become specialized—for example, some become nerve cells, some become muscle cells, and some become skin cells. As this collection of cells takes form, they position themselves to reflect their eventual roles in the body. Cells that are destined to become muscle and intestine position themselves inside the **embryo**, while cells that are destined to become skin position themselves on the outside of the embryo. Axes are established that define the front and back, left and right, and top and bottom of the developing embryo. The organ systems of the body form, and throughout this process, the embryo and then the fetus continue to grow.

Development begins with **fertilization**, the fusion of a sperm cell with an egg cell to produce a genetically unique single cell that ultimately gives rise to every cell in the body. Human development can be divided into three distinct stages:

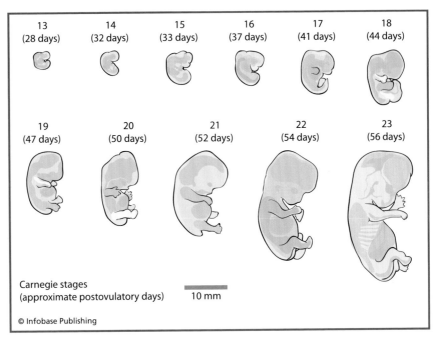

| 13 (28 days) | 14 (32 days) | 15 (33 days) | 16 (37 days) | 17 (41 days) | 18 (44 days) |

| 19 (47 days) | 20 (50 days) | 21 (52 days) | 22 (54 days) | 23 (56 days) |

Carnegie stages
(approximate postovulatory days)        10 mm

© Infobase Publishing

**Figure 1.1** This image shows some stages of human embryonic development. The first two weeks (not shown) are the preembryonic stage; weeks three through eight are the embryonic stage; and from eight weeks (56 days) on is the fetal stage.

preembryonic, embryonic, and fetal. The first two weeks of development are known as the **preembryonic stage**. This stage follows fertilization but precedes the implantation of the embryo into the wall of the mother's uterus. The time from the beginning of week three to the end of week eight is the **embryonic stage** (Figure 1.1). During this time, the embryo undergoes many events that transform it from a mass of cells to human form. From the end of the eighth week until birth, the developing human is called a **fetus**. The fetal stage consists mostly of growth as the inch-long but distinctly human-appearing fetus develops and matures in preparation for birth.

In recent years, there has been remarkable progress in the field of developmental biology. Advances in cell and molecular biology have provided insights into the mechanisms of developmental events that previously could only been observed in wonder. It is amazing to observe the changes in outward physical form of a developing embryo. These outward changes involve a complex array of molecular reaction pathways and cellular processes that must occur at the correct place, in the correct order, and at the proper time for the embryo to develop normally.

The general organization of this book mirrors the order of the developmental events that will be discussed, beginning with the earliest events and highlighting those that take place as the embryo develops human form. The full complexity of the early stages of development are beyond the scope of this book; however, the material that is covered should serve as an introduction and overview of some of the more significant and well-understood events.

# 2

# Development as a Process

DEVELOPMENT BEGINS WITH FERTILIZATION, WHICH PRODUCES a genetically unique single cell called a **zygote**, which is the first cell of the new individual. The zygote gives rise to many cells via repeated cell divisions. The cellular and molecular events that shape this collection of cells into the form of a human represent a complex array of pathways and processes that must interact in very specific ways. Because these pathways and processes are made up of combinations of events, often dependent on one another, their disruption can potentially result in a series of mistakes that can affect the development of the embryo as a whole.

Three hundred years ago, it was believed that human development involved "preformation." According to this theory, individuals developed from fully formed, but extremely miniature, versions of themselves that were present in the sperm or eggs, known as the **gametes**. According to preformationists, every person now existing has existed since the beginning of the human race. Thus people would be somewhat like Russian nesting dolls where each gamete contains a miniature human whose gametes, in turn, contain even more miniature humans and so on. Development, then, would be characterized by the growth and unfolding of these miniature humans. The theory did not deal with the issue of whether the miniature humans were present in the sperm or in the eggs. This created two factions—"ovists" who believed that organisms originated from the egg, while "sperm-ists" believed they originated from the sperm.

As microscopes improved and the field of cell biology advanced, it became clear that development involved a great deal more than preformation. Making use of more powerful microscopes, embryologists learned more about development. Kaspar Friedrich Wolff (1733–1794), who was studying chick development, observed that embryonic structures, such as the heart and kidneys, looked very different from the adult structures into which they develop. If preformation were the mechanism by which development was proceeding, embryonic and adult structures would appear identical, differing only in their size. Wolff also observed that structures such as the heart actually developed anew in each embryo. The development process that Wolff observed, in which structures arise progressively, is known as **epigenesis** (from the Greek word meaning "upon formation"). Interestingly, the idea of epigenesis as the overriding mechanism of development was first recognized and supported by the Greek philosopher Aristotle (384–322 B.C.).

## THE PROCESSES OF EPIGENESIS

If one considers development in a very general way, there are a limited number of general processes that occur as a fertilized egg, as a single cell, becomes a complex multicellular organism, or embryo. In fact, there are five basic processes that contribute to development in general: growth, cell division, differentiation, morphogenesis, and patterning.

Growth is obviously an important component of development as a microscopic single cell becomes a fetus, observable with the naked eye, which, in turn, becomes an even larger newborn baby. In fact, during human fetal development, which proceeds from the beginning of the ninth

(continues on page 17)

## STUDYING MODELS TO GAIN INSIGHTS INTO HUMAN DEVELOPMENT

All multicellular organisms share common elements during their development. Because of this, biologists who study different kinds of organisms not only gain insights into those specific organisms, but often these insights can also be applied to many other organisms, including humans. This is important because it means that organisms similar to humans in certain ways can be studied to gain a better understanding of human biology. It is also important to realize that sometimes the similarities between humans and other organisms may be quite significant while not being overly obvious.

An organism studied for insights into the biology of another organism is called a *model organism*. The work of Kaspar Wolff described earlier in this chapter illustrates the usefulness of studying model organisms for insights into human biology. By observing developing chick embryos under a microscope, Wolff was able to gain a better understanding of how development works in general, and was able to apply his observations, to a certain extent, to humans. When most people think of model organisms used to specifically study human biology, they would likely think of something like a chimpanzee. In fact, medical research involving model organisms sometimes makes use of the unlikeliest of animals. For example, in 2002 and 2006, Nobel prizes in physiology or medicine were awarded to scientists who studied the nematode (roundworm) *Caenorhabditis elegans*. Similarly, in the study of development, amazing advances have been made using the the fruit fly *Drosophila melanogaster* as a model organism. In 1995, the Nobel Prize in Physiology or Medicine was awarded to developmental biologists for their studies on the genes that determine the body plan of *Drosophila*. The principles they discovered also apply to humans and other animals.

Some model organisms that have provided, and continue to provide, insights into human development include mice, frogs, and even fish, as well as the fruit fly, roundworm, and chicks. These diverse organisms can be valuable for a number of reasons. For one thing, most of them are fairly easy and inexpensive to maintain

*(continues on page 16)*

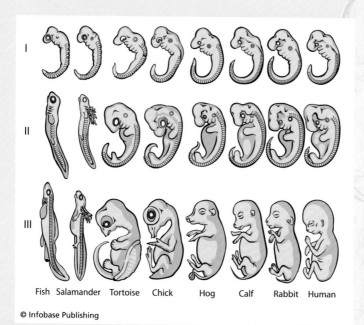

Fish  Salamander  Tortoise  Chick    Hog      Calf    Rabbit  Human

© Infobase Publishing

**Figure 2.1**  Many animals share developmental similarities with humans. By studying these model organisms, we can gain a better understanding of our own development. Here, three stages of development are shown for each organism.

*(continued from page 15)*

in a laboratory. In addition, particularly in relation to the study of development, it is fairly easy to obtain embryos from these organisms. Furthermore, they generally develop much faster than a human (which takes 264 days) or even a chimpanzee (which takes 230 to 240 days). Mice are prolific breeders, and a typical pregnant female will carry as many as 12 embryos that develop from a fertilized egg to a new-born pup in 20 days. Fertilized chicken eggs are easily obtained in great numbers from farms and hatch after approximately 21 days of development. A popular fish model organism, the zebrafish, is not only found in most pet stores, but can produce 100 to 200 embryos per mating, and free-swimming fry develop in just 2 to 3 days.

All of these organisms provide researchers with large numbers of quickly developing embryos that often undergo many of the same developmental processes as a human, only in a much shorter and more easily observable time frame. The ease of observation is another incredibly valuable asset in using many of these animals as models. With the exception of mice, these animals undergo external development (meaning outside of the mother), so that their development can be observed under a microscope as it actually occurs.

It is important to remember that despite the great differences between animals such as a nematode, a fish, and a human, there is also a great deal in common. For example, the embryos of a fish, a bird, and a human appear remarkably similar (Figure 2.1). Based on this, it is clear that a great deal of information may be gleaned by studying the most unlikely animals.

*(continued from page 14)*

week of development until birth, growth is the essential major mechanism taking place. The fetus greatly resembles a miniature adult, although some structures, such as the head, are further advanced in growth than others. During this period, the fetus grows from a mere one inch in length to an average length of 20 inches. Earlier in development, during the preembryonic and embryonic stages, much more than simple growth is occurring.

Fertilization is considered to be the defining step of sexual reproduction. The resulting zygote, which is a single cell, is microscopic in size while a human baby is estimated to consist of 10 trillion cells. For a single-celled zygote to develop into this multicellular organism, it has to undergo cell division, or mitosis. **Mitosis** is a form of cell reproduction in which one cell divides into two cells, which can, in turn, divide to give rise to four cells, which can give rise to eight cells, and so on. Although mitosis can give rise to a vast number of cells, these daughter cells are still identical to each other and to the original, parent, cell. If mitosis and growth were the only mechanisms available for development, the result would be a large mass of identical and uniform cells. However, the human body is not made of a mass of identical cellsm but it is estimated to contain more than 200 different kinds of them, including skin, muscle, nerve, various kinds of blood cells, and **fibroblasts,** which are connective tissue cells (Figure 2.2). As a result of differentiation, these different kinds of cells vary in size, shape, and function.

Differentiation, together with growth and cell division, still do not represent the complete story of development. These processes can give rise to a large mass of cells that are capable of

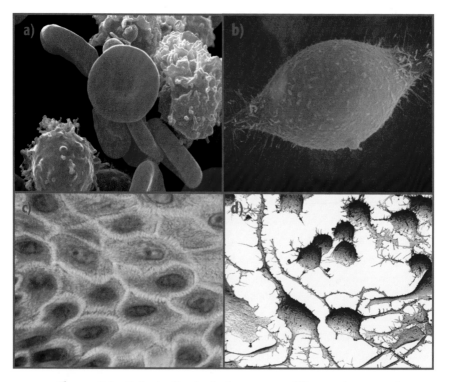

**Figure 2.2** Cells in the body have many different shapes and properties: (a) disc-shaped red blood cells and round white blood cells, (b) a connective tissue cell, or fibroblast, (c) skin cells, and (d) nerve cells, or neurons.

doing different things, but they do not play a role in giving the developing embryo its actual physical appearance. This depends on two other processes: morphogenesis and patterning.

**Morphogenesis** is the process by which the embryo, or regions of the embryo, acquire their specific three-dimensional form. If you look at your hand, you will observe a great deal of form that came about as a result of morphogenesis. Each finger has its own unique shape, as does the hand itself. The form of fingers is different from that of toes because of variations in the morphogenetic pathways that take place during the development of each of these different digits.

The other element that affects the appearance of the embryo is called **patterning**, which is the process by which the body plan is mapped out (Figure 2.3). This includes the establishment of the axes of the body, in which the embryo's

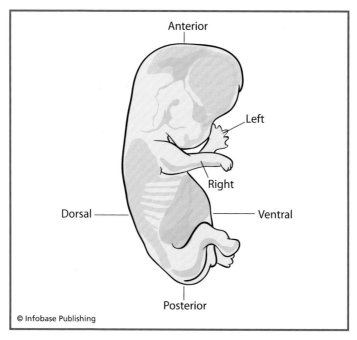

**Figure 2.3**  The major axes of the body are: anterior-posterior, or from top to bottom; dorsal-ventral, or front to back; and left-right.

front and back, head and tail ends, and right and left sides are determined. Patterning also involves the positioning of cells, organs, and structures along the axes. The specification of which vertebra of the skeleton will have attached ribs and which will not is associated with patterning, as is the positioning of the heart and internal organs. Patterning events also position the limbs along the anterior-posterior axis of the body and establish the order of fingers and toes on the hands and feet.

## CONNECTIONS

The processes of growth, cell division, differentiation, patterning, and morphogenesis are all involved in development. Growth and cell division are intimately linked since increase in the number of cells often results in an increase in size. Differentiation is the process by which cells take on specific fates, or will begin to become specialized. Patterning is the process that organizes and positions structures and groups of cells in the organism. Morphogenesis is the process that confers shape and form upon the organism. Although development is clearly very complex, the combination of these five processes produces a human. In fact, these same basic processes are found in virtually all forms of multicellular life, including all animals and plants, as they undergo development.

# 3

# The Cell:
## The Starting Point
## of Development

EVERY HUMAN BODY BEGINS AS A SINGLE CELL, OR ZYGOTE, formed when the father's sperm and mother's egg join. The zygote divides to give rise to two cells that are virtually identical to each other. These two daughter cells can each divide to give rise to four cells, which can then, in turn, divide again. This process allows for an exponential increase in cell number as each round of cell division can potentially double the number of cells produced by the previous division. This type of mechanism involving exponential cell division can be repeated as many times as required to yield enough cells to build a human. Because cells are the basic units of structure and function in humans and all other living things, an understanding of cell structure, organization, and function is crucial to understanding human biology, including development. This chapter will provide a brief introduction to the organization and general functions of a cell.

## ORGANIZATION AND FUNCTIONS
## OF A TYPICAL CELL

In the previous chapter, a number of different kinds of human cells were introduced, such as skin, muscle, and nerve cells.

These cells have many elements in common, but they also have many unique elements. It is the elements that are specific to each cell type that result in the differentiated appearance and function of the specialized cells.

The elements that are common to most human cells are also common to many types of cells in other animals. For example, there are certain activities, such as obtaining nutrients and converting them into cell components and usable energy, which all cells must perform to stay alive. Furthermore, most cells, regardless of their type, use similar mechanisms to perform such functions. Cell biologists refer to these types of mechanisms as housekeeping functions. This degree of commonality further legitimizes the use of model organisms for insights into human biology. Of further interest is the observation that cells that perform similar functions in different organisms are also remarkably similar structurally. For some cell types, it is impossible to tell the difference between a cell from a human, a mouse, or a fish simply by looking at it under a microscope.

A typical animal cell (Figure 3.1) can be compared to a factory containing different kinds of machinery. The outer boundary of an animal cell is called the **plasma membrane**. This membrane separates the material inside the cell from the external environment, much like our skin or the walls of a factory building. Within the cell are many small structures, called **organelles**, which carry out the cell's life activities. An organelle, or "little organ," is a cellular component that has a specific structure and function, much like the organs in an animal. Most organelles are surrounded by a membrane that is similar in general composition, if not identical, to the plasma membrane surrounding the cell. Like the plasma membrane, the function of the organelle's membrane is to separate the organelle's contents from the rest of the environment inside of the cell.

The largest organelle is the **nucleus**, the control center of the cell. The nucleus, which is surrounded by a double

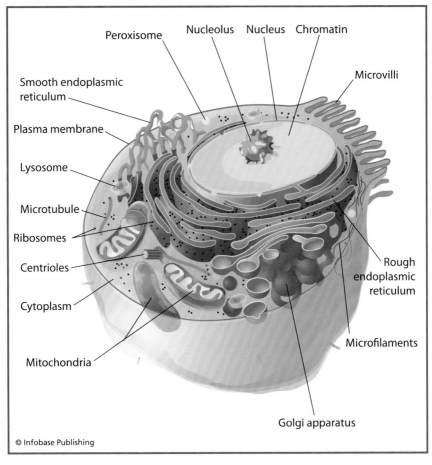

Peroxisome    Nucleolus    Nucleus    Chromatin

Smooth endoplasmic reticulum

Plasma membrane

Lysosome

Microtubule

Ribosomes

Centrioles

Cytoplasm

Mitochondria

Microvilli

Rough endoplasmic reticulum

Microfilaments

Golgi apparatus

© Infobase Publishing

**Figure 3.1** Within the cytoplasm of a typical animal cell are many organelles, including the nucleus, endoplasmic reticulum, Golgi apparatus, and mitochondria. The cytoplasm is a fluid material that fills the area between the nuclear membrane and the plasma membrane.

membrane, contains the **genome**, or the hereditary instructions that are the genetic blueprints for the cell. All of the processes within a cell are controlled by the nucleus, specifically by the **DNA (deoxyribonucleic acid)** contained within the nucleus. DNA also represents the heritable material of the cell. This means that during mitotic cellular reproduction, each daughter cell inherits the same genetic instructions as the parent cell.

This is important because the heritable nature of DNA ensures that each cell that makes up an organism contains essentially the same blueprints.

Adjacent to the nucleus is the **endoplasmic reticulum (ER)**, a network of membranous, flattened sacs and tubes. The membranes of the endoplasmic reticulum closest to the nucleus are covered with subcellular structures called **ribosomes**, giving it a rough appearance. This region is therefore called the *rough endoplasmic reticulum*. Ribosomes are structures that function in protein synthesis, and they are found floating free in the cell cytoplasm and are also attached to the ER. The ER furthest from the nucleus does not have the ribosome covering and is called *smooth endoplasmic reticulum*. Rough endoplasmic reticulum is the site of protein synthesis; smooth endoplasmic reticulum is the region where the cell modifies proteins made in the rough endoplasmic reticulum. The smooth endoplasmic reticulum is also the site of synthesis of steroids, fatty acids, and **phospholipids**, which are the major components of cell membranes.

The **Golgi apparatus**, like the endoplasmic reticulum, is also made up of flattened membranous sacs. The Golgi apparatus stores, modifies, and packages proteins that have been produced in the endoplasmic reticulum and that will eventually be delivered to some other location within or outside of the cell. It also plays an important role in transporting phospholipds around the cell. The Golgi apparatus is very much like a mail room; it reads molecular signals embedded in proteins produced in the rough endoplasmic reticulum (much like zip codes on letters) and uses those signals to send the newly synthesized proteins to their correct destination.

Another organelle found in most cells is the **mitochondrion** (plural, mitochondria). Mitochondria, often called the "power plants" of the cell, provide usable energy for the cell. They are long or oval structures that are surrounded by an outer membrane and an inner membrane that is folded in upon itself. These folds are called *cristae* and the space inside of the mitochondrion is called the *matrix*.

Large molecules in the food we eat are digested, or broken down, into small molecules. These molecules, including sugars, fatty acids, and **amino acids**, are absorbed by the body cells, which can convert them to glucose. The mitochondria break down glucose into carbon dioxide ($CO_2$) and water ($H_2O$). The energy released by this process is used to produce **adenosine triphosphate (ATP)**, a chemical compound that serves as a source of energy for the cell's life processes. The energy stored in ATP is found in bonds that hold the molecule together. When a cell reaction requires energy, ATP is broken down, and the energy released by the breaking of the bonds is used to power the new reaction. ATP and similar molecules are called **activated carriers**.

The breakdown of glucose in mitochondria requires oxygen, which is obtained from the air we breathe. Therefore, these reactions are referred to as oxidation reactions. The carbon dioxide ($CO_2$) and water ($H_2O$) produced by these reactions are exhaled as waste products.

In addition to these relatively large organelles, cells also generally contain a large number of small membrane-bound organelles called *vesicles*. These structures essentially act as storage units inside of the cell. Some vesicles transport materials within the cell, while others store waste products of the cell. Peroxisomes, for example, are a type of vesicle that contains digestive enzymes that break down harmful or toxic materials inside of the cell. These enzymes must be kept separated from the rest of the cell contents so that they do not digest important cell components.

The cell also contains a network of tubular and filamentous proteins that make up the **cytoskeleton**. The cytoskeleton not only provides a protein scaffolding that acts as a support for the cell and maintains its shape, but it also is used by the cell for movement and to move molecules within the cell.

## THE GENOME: THE HEREDITARY BLUEPRINT

A typical cell is a complex collection of components that act together to carry out the cell's life processes. All of these processes are controlled by the nucleus, specifically by the DNA in the nucleus. The DNA is in the form of 46 separate bodies called **chromosomes**. The chromosomes are composed of DNA and protein. The 46 chromosomes actually consist of 23 pairs of chromosomes (Figure 3.2). One complete set of 23 chromosomes (not pairs of chromosomes) constitutes the genome of the cell. With the exception of germ cells, human cells typically contain two genomes—one from the mother and one from the father. The number of sets of chromosomes, or the number of genomes, in the nucleus is referred to as the ploidy, or $n$ number, of the cell. Most human cells contain two sets of the chromosomes and are therefore referred to as **diploid**, or $2n$. The exception to this are human gametes, sperm and ova, which only contain one set of 23 chromosomes and have the **haploid**, or $n$, number of chromosomes. Children receive one genome from each of their parents so that they inherit physical traits from both parents and also from their grandparents.

In addition to carrying the genetic information passed on from parents to offspring, DNA also directs the operations of the cell, including its intercellular interactions. Both roles of DNA are primarily accomplished by its control of protein synthesis. **Proteins** are organic compounds that carry out the majority of cell functions. The importance of proteins in relationship to the functions of the cell is reflected in the observation that proteins make up most of the dry mass of the cell. Proteins make up the cytoskeleton, which gives the cell its shape and the ability to move; enzymes are proteins that catalyze most of the chemical reactions in the cell; specialized proteins act as channels and pumps in cell membranes to control the passage of molecules into and out of the cell and into and out of organelles; hormones and other proteins act as messengers, allowing communication between differents parts of a cell

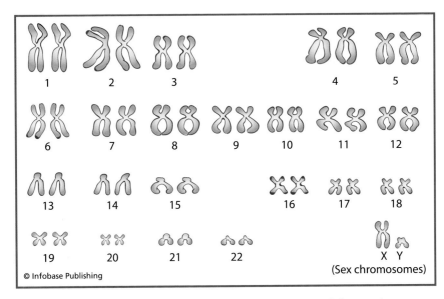

**Figure 3.2** A human karyotype—an image of a full set of 46 chromosomes from a cell arranged according to their size and shape—is shown here. Notice that all the chromosomes are in matched pairs except for the X and Y chromosomes, the sex chromosomes. The cells of females contain two X chromosomes while the cells of males have one X chromosome and one Y chromosome.

and between cells. Clearly, proteins play important roles in cellular functions. The question now is how DNA, which carries the instructions for synthesis of the cell's proteins, implements these instructions.

## FROM GENOTYPE TO PHENOTYPE: FOLLOWING THE BLUEPRINT

To understand how DNA acts as the blueprint for a cell and for an organism requires some understanding of the molecular nature of DNA. In a cell, DNA typically exists in the form of double-stranded molecules. The two strands wind around each, creating a structure called the double helix. Each strand of DNA is made up of a long chain of molecules called **nucleotides**. Nucleotides are made up of three subunits:

a nitrogen-containing base, a deoxyribose sugar molecule, and a phosphate group. The nitrogen-containing base is joined to the deoxyribose molecule, which, in turn, is joined to the phosphate group. Nucleotides are joined together in such a way that deoxyribose sugars and phosphate groups form alternating units that make up a flexible, ribbonlike backbone, much like the sides of a ladder. Extending away from this backbone, like the rungs of a ladder, are the bases. There are four different bases in DNA: adenine, cytosine, guanine, and thymine, commonly abbreviated A, C, G, and T, respectively. An important characteristic of these bases is that they bond together in only one way—that is, adenine and thymine bond together and guanine and cytosine bond together. The interactions of these pairs of bases hold the two strands of DNA together to form the double helix. The bases make up the "rungs" of the DNA "ladder" (Figure 3.3). An adenine on one strand bonds to a thymine on the opposite, or complementary, strand, and a guanine on one strand bonds to a cytosine on the complementary strand.

The sequences of the bases along a strand of DNA are the code for the production of a specific protein. Regions of DNA that are able to code for a protein are called **genes**. All the genes in an organism are its **genotype**. Interestingly, most of the chromosome material is not made up of genes, nor are all genes active at all times. Of the approximately three billion nucleotides that make up the human genome, less than 2% code for the production of protein. The current estimate for the number of genes in the human genome is between 20,000 and 25,000. The genes are distributed throughout the genome, often separated by great stretches of noncoding DNA. Some of the noncoding regions are known to act as regulatory regions. They are areas of DNA that essentially act as molecular docks that can be bound by factors, such as proteins, that dictate when genes are active or inactive. However, many of the noncoding regions have no discernible function, and are sometimes referred to as "junk DNA."

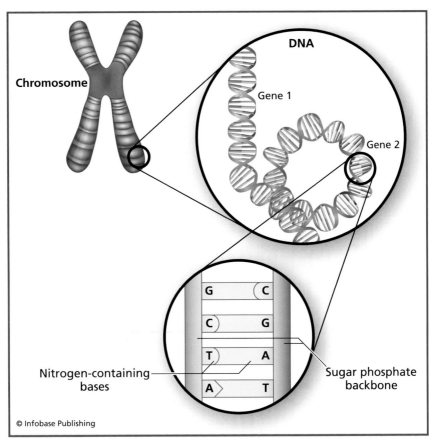

**Figure 3.3** DNA contains a cell's hereditary information. DNA molecules are in the form of a double helix, rather like a twisted ladder. The flexible ribbons of the DNA strands represent the sugar phosphate backbone, and the interactions that hold the two strands together are a result of a base on each strand pairing with a complementary base on the opposite strand. The base pairings are represented as the rungs holding the strands together.

DNA does not leave the cell nucleus, but protein synthesis occurs in the cell cytoplasm. (The cytoplasm is the material that fills the space between the nuclear membrane and the cell's bounding plasma membrane.) For the information coded in the bases of DNA to be used by the cell, it must

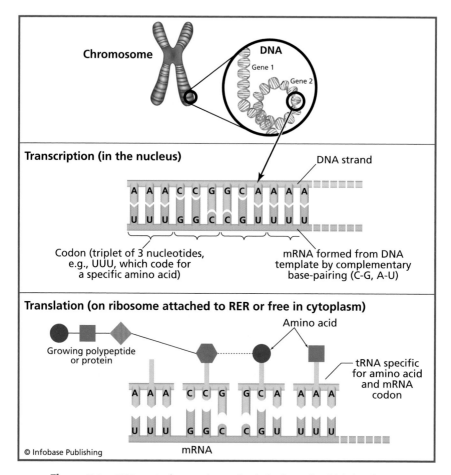

**Figure 3.4**   DNA controls protein synthesis in the cell, which involves the processes of transcription and translation. In transcription, the double strand of DNA separates, and one strand acts as a template to produce a strand of mRNA. The code in the mRNA strand is then used as a set of instructions for ribosomes to translate this information into a strand of amino acids (the second part of the process).

first reach the cytoplasm, which requires two processes. **Transcription**, the first process, involves a copying of the sequence of the coding region of a gene into a molecule of **ribonucleic acid**, or **RNA** (Figure 3.4). RNA, like DNA, is made up of chains of nucleotides, but with a slightly different sugar component. The bases in RNA are the same as the bases as DNA except that a base called uracil, abbreviated U, replaces thymine. Uracil is similar to thymine and bonds with adenine. The process of transcription is initiated when a large number of proteins collect near the beginning of the coding region of a gene. These proteins, known as the *general transcriptional machinery*, act together to initiate transcription. The actual process of transcription involves a subset of these proteins tracking along the coding region of the DNA molecule. As the proteins do this, they copy the sequence of nucleotides of the gene into a strand of RNA, except that uracil replaces thymine.

By analogy, if the DNA represents the blueprint, RNA represents a copy of this blueprint. Upon completion of the transcription process, the RNA copy passes out of the nucleus. Because this RNA carries the genetic information from the nucleus to the cytoplasm, it is called *messenger RNA*, or *mRNA*. The nucleus, therefore, can be considered to be something like a reference library that contains all the information the cell requires to function properly. The genome represents all the books in the library, but they cannot be checked out. The process of transcription, then, is analgous to photocopying a library book so that the information in that book may be removed, while the original source of the information is kept safely in the library. The mRNA is that photocopy.

The second process in protein synthesis is called **translation**. In translation, the information encoded in the base sequence of the mRNA molecule is translated into the amino acid sequence of a protein. Each amino acid is specified by a particular sequence of three nucleotides in the mRNA. For example, the sequence AAA specifies that the amino acid lysine should be inserted into the forming protein. The organelles that function in translation are the ribosomes, which bind to an mRNA molecule. The ribosome moves along the mRNA strand and, following the coding rules, translates the information from the nucleotide language to the language of amino acids. Amino acids from the cell cytoplasm are carried to the mRNA by another kind of RNA called *transfer RNA*, or *tRNA*.

Proteins are made up of chains of twenty different kinds of amino acids. Amino acids have different biochemical properties based upon their particular molecular structure. Different proteins are made up of different sequences of the twenty amino acids. Based on their differences in sequence of amino acids and the different biochemical properties of each of these amino

## CLONING BY NUCLEAR TRANSFER

Recently, the possibility of producing animals asexually, or by cloning, has received a great deal of media attention. In 1997, biologists in Scotland announced the birth of Dolly the sheep. Dolly was the first mammal cloned from an adult cell. The implications of Dolly have been far reaching, particularly because the technique used to clone her can potentially be applied to many organisms, including humans. Sexual reproduction involves combining genetic information from two parents, thus creating a unique individual. Cloning, or asexual reproduction, involves the production of an organism that is genetically identical to an existing individual. The technique used to produce Dolly is called *nuclear transplantation,* or *somatic cell nuclear transfer.*

Nuclear transfer requires an egg cell and the genetic material from a **somatic cell**. A somatic cell is any cell from an organism except for **germ cells** (which give rise to sperm or eggs). The actual nuclear transfer involves removing the nucleus from the egg cell and replacing it with a nucleus taken from a somatic cell of another individual. Instead of genetic material from two individual parents being combined to produce a zygote, the zygote contains the genetic material of only one individual, the donor who already exists! After the donor genetic material has been introduced into the egg cell, the cell is stimulated to begin development either chemically or by an electric shock. The embryo that begins to develop can potentially grow and develop for a number of days in the

acids, the proteins have different structures that enable them to perform different functions. Proteins are involved in virtually all of the cell's functions, and they are major structural components as well. By extension, it can be said that since animals and plants are large collections of cells, proteins account for the structure and functions in of the organism. The appearance of an organism is its **phenotype**. The phenotype is determined by the genotype, which functions in the processes of transcription and translation. The environment can also affect phenotype.

laboratory, but continued development requires that this preembryo be implanted into a surrogate mother. The individual who develops from this embryo, instead of representing a combination of the genetic traits of two parents, will be virtually genetically identical to the individual who provided the donor genetic material.

The question of how this technique could benefit society remains to be answered. Human cloning could prove beneficial. It has been proposed that this technique could potentially be used to help infertile couples to have children or to clone a child who has died. There is even interest in using this technology to clone pets. In addition, it could help people who suffer from degenerative diseases such as Alzheimer's disease, Parkinson's disease, Huntington's disease, and ALS (Lou Gehrig's disease). Cloning could potentially help treat diseases by creating a clone of the individual suffering from a particular disease, and then using stem cells from the embryo to treat the disease (stem cells and their uses are discussed in greater detail in Chapter 4). A number of biotech companies, including Advanced Cell Technology (ACT), based in Massachusetts, and Stemagen, based in California, have successfully created cloned human preembryos with an eye toward using the technology to produce stem cells. The process of cloning, however, is still incredibly inefficient, and much research still needs to be done to perfect this technique. For example, Dolly was the only clone born from a study that began with 277 zygotes that were created by nuclear transfer.

## CONNECTIONS

A typical cell is a complex collection of components that act together to carry out cell functions. The endoplasmic reticulum produces materials needed by the cell, the Golgi apparatus sends these materials to where they are needed, and the mitochondria provide the energy. In addition, there are structures that store substances, separating them from the cell's interior, and other structures that act as scaffolding and enable cell movements. All cell processes are controlled by the nucleus, specifically by the DNA contained within the nucleus. Cellular functions are controlled by specific regions of DNA called genes that collectively represent the genotype. The genotype controls the appearance and functions of the cell, or the phenotype, via two processes: transcription of an RNA copy of a gene and the subsequent translation of this RNA copy into protein.

The process of development extends the cellular relationship between genotype and phenotype to construct an organism. During development, different sets of genes are expressed in different cells. This differential gene expression can lead to developmental events such as differentiation, patterning, and morphogenesis. Differential expression of subsets of genes in a cell can also result in that cell entering mitosis.

# 4

# The First Steps to Multicellularity

IN THE LAST CHAPTER, THE ORGANIZATION OF A BASIC CELL was introduced. Also discussed were some of the basic mechanisms that generally take place in every cell, essentially in order for a cell to operate normally. These mechanisms were associated with specific organelles, such as the nucleus acting as the genetic control center of the cell. The concepts of transcription and translation were also introduced as the two processes that allow the genotype, or the DNA of the cell, to control the phenotype, or the appearance of the cell. Many of the concepts that were introduced will appear throughout this book. Understanding them will be important because they will form a basis for understanding more widespread developmental mechanisms. In other words, to understand how development is occurring at a certain level of the organism will require an understanding of what is happening at both the molecular and cellular levels in that organism.

## FERTILIZATION

Sperm and eggs, or gametes, are specialized cells that differ from the somatic cells that make up the other cells of the human body. Somatic cells are diploid, which means that they contain two copies of the genetic information, one from each parent. Sperm and egg cells are derived from germ cells by a special type of cell division called **meiosis**. As a result of meiosis, which divides the genetic material in half, sperm and egg cells are haploid—they contain only one copy of the full genetic information. Most human cells are diploid: They contain two genomes, or two copies of the genetic information. The 46 chromosomes found in the nucleus of a diploid cell are actually 23 pairs of chromosomes. One of the chromosomes from each pair comes from the mother and the other comes from the father. Thus, when gametes are produced, it must be in such a way that the genetic information is reduced to half, so that they contain only 23 chromosomes, one copy of each chromosome. In this way, fertilization restores the full, diploid chromosome number to the zygote, the first cell of a new individual. The combining of genetic information from two individuals is the biological definition of sexual reproduction, and it is because of this that children inherit traits from each parent.

In human sexual reproduction, the process leading up to fertilization typically involves a number of sperm cells ejaculated by the father coming into contact with the much larger egg cell, or **oocyte** (Figure 4.1a). The oocyte develops in and is released from one of the mother's ovaries. The oocyte is surrounded by a protective covering called the **zona pellucida**. When a sperm comes into contact with the oocyte, the tip of the sperm head, called the **acrosome**, releases an enzyme that digests a region of the zona pellucida. This forms a path through the zona pellucida for the sperm to pass through. Once the sperm makes its way though the zona pellucida, it comes into contact with the plasma membrane surrounding the oocyte, and the membranes surrounding the sperm and oocyte cells fuse. This fusion of sperm and oocyte membranes allows the nucleus of the sperm to enter the oocyte. The fusion of a single sperm with the oocyte also produces a change in the

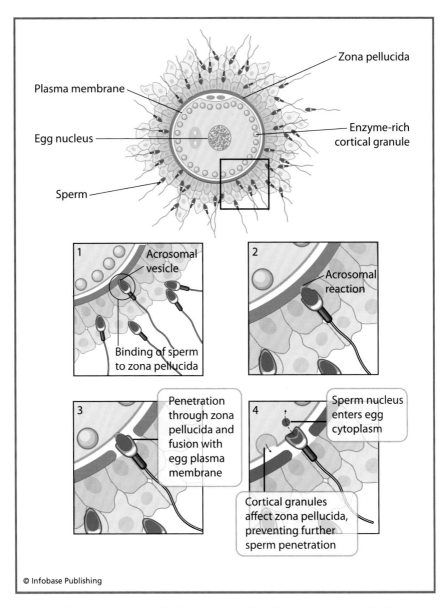

**Figure 4.1a**   In fertilization, the sperm first binds to the zona pelludica of the egg. Then the acrosome releases an enzyme that digests the zona pellucida, allowing the sperm to enter the egg. Finally, cortical granules prevent any additional sperm from penetrating the zona pellucida.

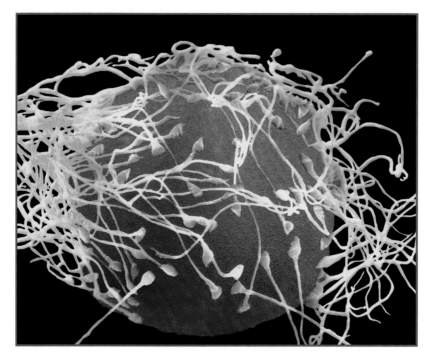

**Figure 4.1b** A scanning electron micrograph of an oocyte being fertilized is shown here. Note that although several sperm are competing for a chance to fertilize the egg, only one can enter.

zona pellucida that prevents any other sperm from entering (Figure 4.1b). Fertilization is considered to be complete when the haploid nucleus from the sperm fuses with the haploid egg nucleus. This fusion creates the diploid nucleus of the zygote.

## CLEAVAGE

After fertilization, the zygote begins to undergo development. This single cell eventually gives rise to every cell in the new individual. During the first four days after fertilization, the stage known as **cleavage**, the principle developmental mechanism is cell division, or mitosis. Cleavage involves a series of cell divisions that are not accompanied by any growth. Essentially what is occurring is that the relatively large zygote

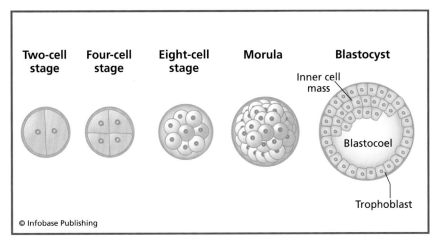

**Figure 4.2**  Preembryonic development involves several rounds of cell division. Cleavage involves five synchronous cell divisions that give rise to a 32-cell morula. The cells of the morula continue to divide and rearrange themselves into a more rounded and hollow ball-like blastocyst.

is subdivided into smaller and smaller cells whose combined size is approximately the same as the zygote. During this time, approximately five cell divisions occur, resulting in 32 cells. These 32 cells are essentially identical to one another and are all clustered together in a single mass. This mass of cells is called the **morula**, which literally means "little mulberry" and is based on the clustered appearance of the cells at this stage (Figure 4.2). This process is fueled by nutrients present in the original oocyte. These nutrients are not sufficient, however, to supply the entire developmental process. Additional nutrients must be obtained from the mother, which requires a connection between the preembryo and the mother.

## DEVELOPMENT OF THE EXTRAEMBRYONIC TISSUES

The events of cleavage, the development of the morula, and the subsequent attachment to the mother, or *implantation*, are commonly referred to as the *preembryonic* stage of development. Many of the cells of the preembryo do not actually contribute to the embryo itself. Instead, these cells form the extraembryonic tissues, such as the placenta. Around the fourth day after fertilization, cells of the preembryo continue to divide, but they also begin to undergo differentiation and morphogenesis. During the next several days, cells present on the outside of the preembryo begin to differentiate, or take on specific characteristics. In addition, cells of the preembryo begin to make morphogenic movements, as the shape of the preembryo changes from the mulberry-shaped morula to a more rounded, ball-like shape. This ball of cells is called the **blastocyst**. If a blastocyst is cut in half, the inside shows three distinct regions: a hollow cavity, called the **blastocoel**; a collection of cells called the **inner cell mass**; and a cell layer called the **trophoblast**, which makes up the outer sphere of the blastocyst.

The cells of the trophoblast mediate the implantation of the blastocyst into the uterine wall of the mother. Implantation takes place during the second week of development. This process begins when the blastocyst comes into contact with the lining of the uterus, which is called *endometrium*. The thickness of the endometrium varies with the stages of the menstrual cycle, and it is thickest during the part of the cycle when fertilization is most likely to occur. When the blastocyst comes into contact with the endometrium, the trophoblast cells surrounding the blastocyst secrete digestive enzymes that break down the endometrial cells. The part of the trophoblast that grows into the endometrium is called the *syncytiotrophoblast*. The breakdown of the endometrium creates a path that allows the blastocyst to burrow into the endometrial tissue.

After implantation, cells of the trophoblast continue to divide and differentiate, eventually giving rise to the **chorion**, the outermost layer of cells surrounding the implanted embryo. This layer of cells produces hormones to support the early pregnancy. The chorion also produces and releases digestive enzymes that break down the mother's endometrial cells and capillaries in the area surrounding the embryo. This digestion of capillaries leads to their rupture and the formation of cavities filled with blood in the vicinity of the embryo. The chorion also extends projections into these blood-filled cavities to allow the embryo to obtain nutrients and oxygen from them while excreting wastes. The structure that is formed by the chorion, its projections into the endometrium, and the endometrium itself is called the **placenta**.

## THE EARLY EMBRYO: THE INNER CELL MASS
The embryo develops from the inner cell mass of the blasto-cyst. During preembryonic development, the cells of the inner cell mass are essentially equivalent to each other. If the inner cell mass is divided, each cell or collection of cells that results has the potential to form a complete embryo. In fact, it is just

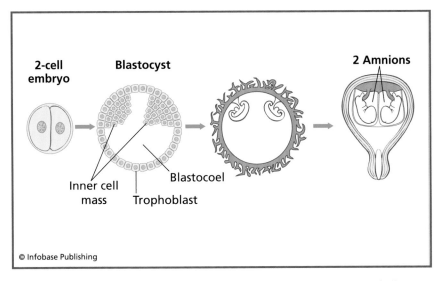

© Infobase Publishing

**Figure 4.3**  The division of the inner cell mass can result in each half giving rise to an embryo. Such an event can lead to the development of monozygotic, or identical, twins.

## STEM CELLS

Human embryonic stem cells were first isolated in 1998 by James Thomson at the University of Wisconsin-Madison. Embryonic stem cells are obtained by harvesting cells from the inner cell mass of human blastocysts. This process destroys the preembryo, which is the principal reason that so much controversy surrounds the ethics of using embryonic stem cells. The primary source of blastocysts is excess preembryos from in vitro fertilization (IVF). IVF allows infertile couples to produce children. This technique involves removing a number of oocytes and sperm from the parents and mixing these germ cells in a dish in the laboratory. Typically, many oocytes are fertilized during this procedure, with only a subset of them being implanted into the mother. The remaining preembryos are generally frozen. If these frozen preembryos are not needed, the parents may consent to donate them for research. Upon their isolation, the stem cells can be cultured in the laboratory, potentially providing an indefinite supply. As discussed in the previous chapter, there is also a great deal of promise for generating embryonic stem cells using theraputic cloning.

With continued research, stem cells may become a powerful tool for treatment of many diseases, particularly degenerative diseases. The cells of the inner cell mass are pluripotent, or have the potential to become any cell type or tissue that is found in a human. Potential uses for embryonic stem cells include treatment for diseases such as Alzheimer's disease, Parkinson's disease, Huntington's disease, and ALS (Lou Gehrig's disease), as well as spinal cord injuries. In fact, there has been some very encouraging experimental evidence for the successful treatment of spinal cord injuries with stem cells in rats. Embryonic stem cells are also potentially useful for treating diseases and injuries that damage part of an organ or tissue. For example, when a heart attack results in the death of a portion of the heart muscle, stem cells could be injected into damaged or injured tissue and be induced to differentiate to repair that tissue.

such a division that can lead to the development of monozygotic, or identical, twins (Figure 4.3). The cells of the inner cell mass are often referred to as **pluripotent cells** because any one of them has the capacity to form any type of human cell or tissue. During the first several weeks of development, the cells of the inner cell mass are pluripotent largely because they have not yet undergone differentiation. After approximately the first two weeks of development, which largely involves the development of the extraembryonic tissues, the inner cell mass begins a program of rapid growth, differentiation, and morphogenesis that lasts for approximately six weeks. The period of development beginning at the start of the third week and finishing near the end of the eighth week is when the developing human is called an embryo.

## CONNECTIONS

Following fertilization, the zygote undergoes a number of cell divisions during a stage called cleavage. This process results in a mass of relatively uniform cells. The cells located on the outside of this mass become the trophoblast. This gives rise to the extraembryonic tissues, such as the placenta, and thus plays an important role in implantation and the subsequent connection between embryo and mother that enables the embryo to obtain nutrients and dispose of wastes. Cells located in the inside of the preembryo give rise to the inner cell mass, which in turn gives rise to every type of cell or tissue that makes up a human. Because of the versatility of these cells, they have the potential to be powerful tools for research as well as for potentially treating a large number of diseases.

# 5

# The Developing Embryo

CHAPTER 4 DISCUSSED THE EARLY DEVELOPMENTAL EVENTS that result in the implantation of the preembryo into the uterine lining of the mother. That chapter also discussed the development of the inner cell mass. The pluripotent cells of the inner cell mass soon begin to acquire specific identities, making possible the development of the actual embryo.

During the second week after fertilization, while the trophoblast is involved in implantation, inside the blastocyst, a thin layer of cells called the *hypoblast* delaminates from the inner cell mass (Figure 5.1). These cells migrate and divide to line the blastocoel; this newly lined cavity is called the yolk sac. Like the trophoblast, the yolk sac is considered to be an extraembryonic tissue. As development proceeds, the yolk sac becomes an extension of the developing gut of the embryo. As the hypoblast is forming, the remaining cells of the inner cell mass become known as the **epiblast**. Another layer of cells delaminates from the epiblast. This occurs on the side of the epiblast that is opposite from the hypoblast. This forms a second cavity that will come to be filled with amniotic fluid. This fluid-filled amniotic cavity insulates and protects the developing fetus. Later in development, as the kidneys form, the fetus will urinate into

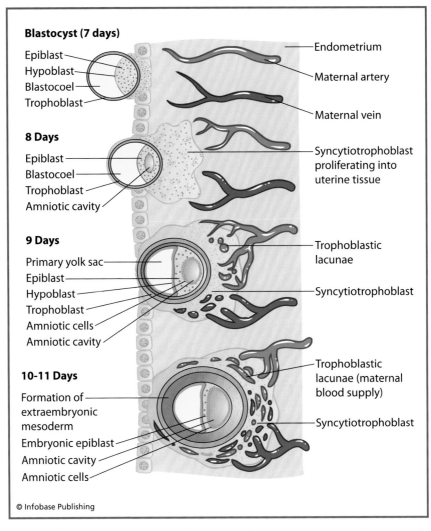

**Blastocyst (7 days)**

Epiblast
Hypoblast
Blastocoel
Trophoblast

Endometrium
Maternal artery
Maternal vein

**8 Days**

Epiblast
Blastocoel
Trophoblast
Amniotic cavity

Syncytiotrophoblast
proliferating into
uterine tissue

**9 Days**

Primary yolk sac
Epiblast
Hypoblast
Trophoblast
Amniotic cells
Amniotic cavity

Trophoblastic
lacunae

Syncytiotrophoblast

**10-11 Days**

Formation of
extraembryonic
mesoderm
Embryonic epiblast
Amniotic cavity
Amniotic cells

Trophoblastic
lacunae (maternal
blood supply)

Syncytiotrophoblast

© Infobase Publishing

**Figure 5.1**  During preembryonic development prior to gastrulation, the trophoblast is involved in implanting into the endometrium of the mother's uterus. As this is occurring, the cells of the inner cell mass continue to divide and will give rise to some extraembryonic tissues as well as the embryo.

the amniotic cavity where these wastes will then be removed through exchange with the mother via the extraembryonic tissues. The band of cells that remains in the inner cell mass, and which is now positioned between the yolk sac and amniotic cavity, is called the **embryonic disc**. This small collection of cells, approximately 0.1 to 0.2 millimeters in length, will give rise to the embryo.

## GASTRULATION

The first major developmental event that the embryonic disc undergoes is **gastrulation**. During this process, the cells of the embryo undergo significant movements as they rearrange themselves. These movements ultimately lead to the establishment of the basic tissue types and the generation of organs. Gastrulation also results in the establishment of the general layout of the body plan. Because of its broad-reaching impact on development, this stage is critically important for the continued development of the embryo. The significance of this developmental event is so great that the embryologist Lewis Wolpert said, "It is not birth, marriage, or death, but gastrulation which is truly the most important time of your life."

Before gastrulation, the embryonic disc is essentially made up of two layers of cells and is described as *bilaminar* (Figure 5.2). As gastrulation begins, cells on the surface of the disc that face away from the yolk sac, the epiblast, begin moving toward the center line of the disc. These movements begin at one end, or pole, of the disc. This end, or region, of the embryonic disc will eventually become the posterior end of the embryo.

As the cells from either side of this surface of the embryonic disc reach the center midline, they collide. The midline where these collisions occur takes on an irregular appearance relative to the rest of the surface of the embryonic disc. The sheets of cells converging at the midline of the embryonic disc give rise to a line running down the center of the disc. This line is called the **primitive streak**. As cells collide at the midline to give rise to the primitive streak, they are forced out along the

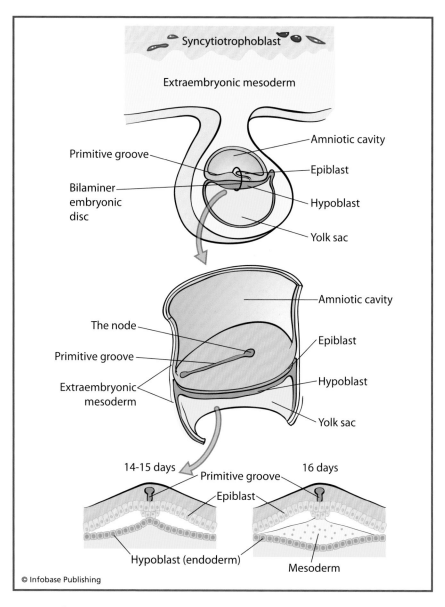

**Figure 5.2** During gastrulation, the cells of the embryo undergo extensive movement and rearrangement to convert the bilaminar embryonic disc into a more complex structure made up of the three distinct germ layers.

axis being created along that midline. This causes the primitive streak to elongate along the axis of the midline towards the opposite pole of the embryo. By analogy, the primitive streak is somewhat similar to toothpaste being squeezed out of a tube. The squeezing causes the toothpaste particles in the tube to collide, which ultimately results in the forcing of some particles through the end of the tube.

In the embryo, cells colliding at the presumptive posterior end of the embryo, at the primitive streak, will force some cells to move perpendicular to their original direction of motion as they are squeezed together. This process causes the primitive streak to extend along the midline toward what will become the anterior end of the embryo. By the time this process is completed, the anterior-posterior axis and the dorsal midline have been established.

At the apex of the extending primitive streak, a structure called the **node** develops. The node, a knotlike structure, develops largely as a result of cells initially piling up in this region before being forced to move anteriorly. In organisms other than humans, the node is called Hensen's node, after its discoverer, the German anatomist and physiologist Viktor Hensen (1835–1924).

As cells move across the surface of the embryo and collide to form the extending primitive streak, cells at the primitive streak also pass into the disc. These cells move inward and pass through the primitive streak, which is now known as the **primitive groove**. Once the cells enter the embryonic disc through the primitive groove, they spread out between the two cell layers that make up the disc, the top epiblast and bottom hypoblast. These two cell movements are the principle events associated with gastrulation. These cell movements transform the bilaminar embryonic disc into a more complex structure made up of three distinct layers. Collectively, these populations of cells are known as the three **germ layers**: the ectoderm, the mesoderm, and the endoderm.

## THE GERM LAYERS: ENDODERM, MESODERM, AND ECTODERM

The germ layers represent the three different cell types that will continue to differentiate during development to give rise to the more than 200 different types of cells that make up a human (Figure. 5.3). The **endoderm** lineage represents the innermost layer of cells following gastrulation. These cells are the first to migrate through the primitive streak and the adult cells that they will give rise to include those that will make up the gut, the liver, and the lungs. The cells that migrate

## STUDYING GASTRULATION

Studying gastrulation in humans is difficult because of the small size of the embryo during this process and because of the small number of human embryos that are available for study. A number of collections of preserved human embryos do exist, however, and these collections can be used to gain some insights into human development. In addition, early developmental events, such as cleavage, can be observed under a microscope during in vitro fertilization procedures at fertility clinics, before the injection of the preembryos into the mother. Observing a gastrulating human embryo in this manner, however, is virtually impossible because gastrulation occurs after implantation and, thus, inside the uterus. What is known about gastrulation in humans, then, is gleaned from a combination of information from embryos in collections as well as from observing model organisms, such as mice and chick embryos. The cell movements that take place during gastrulation in the chick are remarkably similar to those that take place in mammals, including humans. Furthermore, in chick embryos the cell movements can actually be observed as they occur by cutting a window into the egg and observing development under a microscope. Using observations from model organisms, the events of human gastrulation have been pieced together. Combining data from different sources illustrates the power of utilizing model organisms to study development.

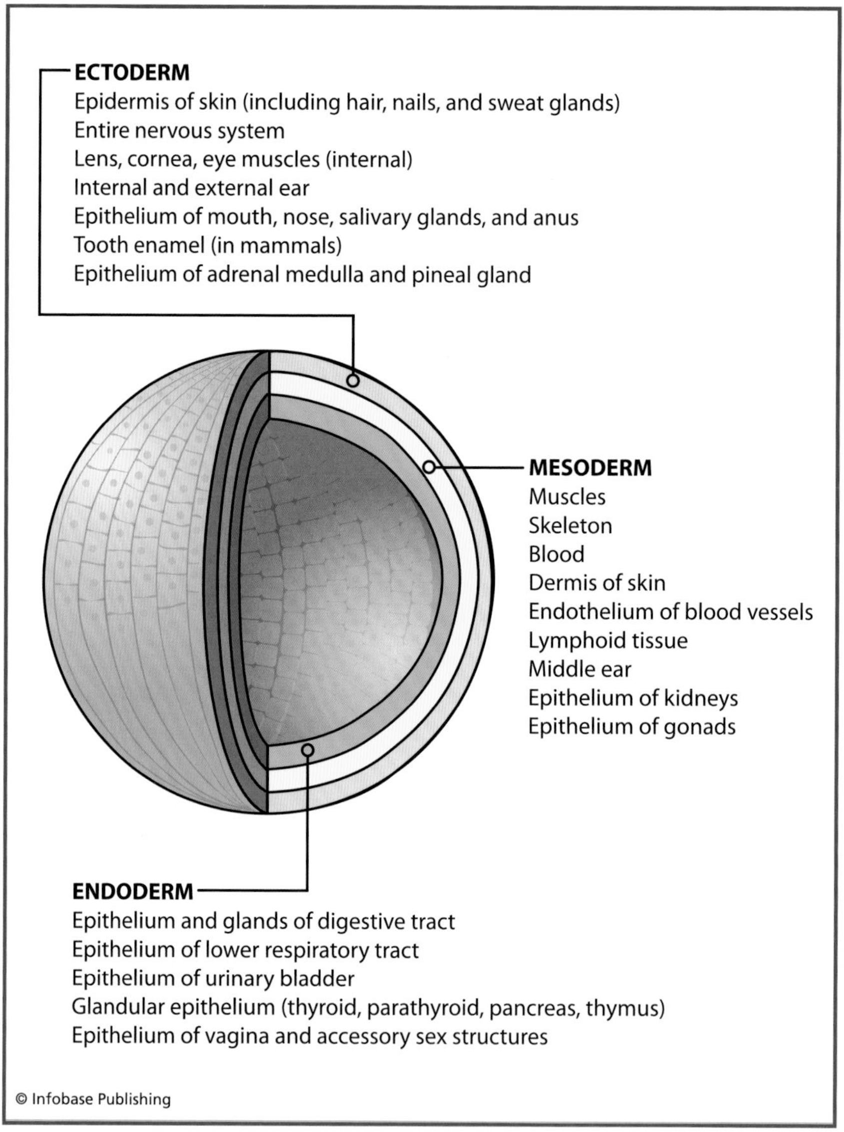

**ECTODERM**
Epidermis of skin (including hair, nails, and sweat glands)
Entire nervous system
Lens, cornea, eye muscles (internal)
Internal and external ear
Epithelium of mouth, nose, salivary glands, and anus
Tooth enamel (in mammals)
Epithelium of adrenal medulla and pineal gland

**MESODERM**
Muscles
Skeleton
Blood
Dermis of skin
Endothelium of blood vessels
Lymphoid tissue
Middle ear
Epithelium of kidneys
Epithelium of gonads

**ENDODERM**
Epithelium and glands of digestive tract
Epithelium of lower respiratory tract
Epithelium of urinary bladder
Glandular epithelium (thyroid, parathyroid, pancreas, thymus)
Epithelium of vagina and accessory sex structures

**Figure 5.3**  During development, cells form three germ layers. The ectoderm is the outermost layer, the mesoderm is the middle layer, and the endoderm is the innermost layer. Examples of the types of cells derived from each germ layer are listed here.

into the embryo later and that position themselves between the endoderm and surface layer become the **mesoderm**. The adult cells that the mesoderm will give rise to include those that make up the skeleton and skeletal muscle, the heart, the blood, and the kidneys. The cells that remain on the surface of the embryo become the **ectoderm**. The adult cells that this lineage of cells gives rise to include the skin and central nervous system.

## CONNECTIONS

During the process of gastrulation, the cells of the embryo undergo significant morphogenetic movements that result in the establishment of the germ layers. The layers continue to differentiate during development to give rise to more than 200 different types of cells that make up a human. Each of the germ layers is positioned in a manner consistent with the body plan of a human. The ectoderm, which gives rise to the skin, is positioned on the outer surface of the embryo. Beneath the ectoderm, the mesoderm is positioned where it will give rise to cells such as those that will make muscle and bone. The mesoderm, in turn, overlays the endoderm, the lineage that will give rise to the digestive system. During this time, the future axes also become established. Thus, after gastrulation, much of the future body plan of the developing human has been mapped out. The next chapter will focus on how the layout of the body is further refined and how the ectodermal lineage gives rise to the central nervous system.

# 6

# Development of the Central Nervous System

DURING GASTRULATION, THE CELLS OF THE EMBRYO UNDERGO significant morphogenetic movements that result in the establishment of the three germ layers. The relationship between the positions of the germ layers after gastrulation and the eventual fates of the cells of each of the germ layers makes sense in terms of the internal and external organization of the human body. The external body plan is essentially based on the three axes—anterior-posterior, dorsal-ventral, and left-right. The discussion of gastrulation in the previous chapter described how this developmental event contributes to the establishment of both the anterior-posterior and dorsal-ventral axes.

Gastrulation also, and significantly, defines the internal and cellular organization of the body. If one imagines what a cross section through a human body looks like in a very general sense, it would likely resemble something similiar to that shown in Figure 6.1. Running through the body, along the anterior-posterior axis, is the gut. The gut is essentially a tube that runs from the mouth, through the digestive system, to the anus. The lining of the gut and the structures associated with it, such as the stomach, intestines, and liver, are all derived from the endoderm.

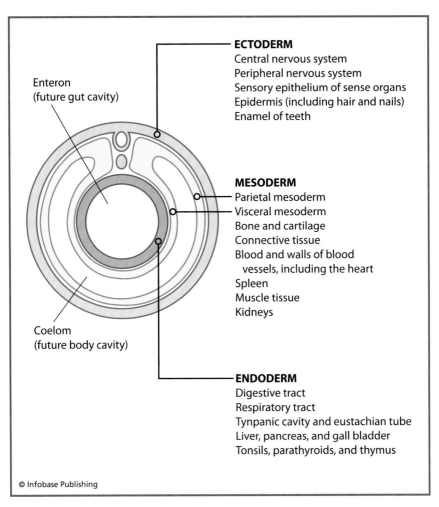

Enteron
(future gut cavity)

**ECTODERM**
Central nervous system
Peripheral nervous system
Sensory epithelium of sense organs
Epidermis (including hair and nails)
Enamel of teeth

**MESODERM**
Parietal mesoderm
Visceral mesoderm
Bone and cartilage
Connective tissue
Blood and walls of blood
   vessels, including the heart
Spleen
Muscle tissue
Kidneys

Coelom
(future body cavity)

**ENDODERM**
Digestive tract
Respiratory tract
Tynpanic cavity and eustachian tube
Liver, pancreas, and gall bladder
Tonsils, parathyroids, and thymus

© Infobase Publishing

**Figure 6.1**  Shown here is a diagrammatic representation showing the relative positions of the three germ layers and their derivatives. The enteron and coelom form the gut and body cavities, respectively. The ectoderm forms the central and peripheral nervous systems, as well as skin cells (epidermis). The mesoderm forms many essential organs, including bone, blood, heart, spleen, and kidneys. The endoderm forms the remaining organs, as well as the digestive and respiratory tracts.

Immediately surrounding the endodermal derivatives in the body is the musculature, the skeleton, and the circulatory system (the heart, blood vessels, and blood), all derivatives of the mesoderm. In terms of gastrulation, this makes sense as this process places the mesoderm immediately surrounding the endoderm. Finally, the cells that surround the mesodermal and endodermal derivatives come from the ectoderm. Just as it makes sense that the mesoderm would surround the endoderm, it also makes sense that the ectoderm that is present on the surface following gastrulation would give rise to the skin, which represents the surface surrounding the body.

## NEURULATION

The ectoderm, in addition to giving rise to the skin, also gives rise to the central nervous system—the brain and spinal cord. The development of these complex structures is not easy to describe in terms of the cellular rearrangements associated with gastrulation. This is because **neurulation**, or the early development of the central nervous system, involves additional cell movements following gastrulation. Neurulation forms the neural tube, a structure that runs along the anterior-posterior axis on the dorsal side of the embryo. This tube eventually gives rise to the brain at the most anterior region and, more posteriorly, the spinal cord.

To a certain extent, neurulation actually begins while gastrulation is still in progress. During gastrulation, cells migrate through the entire length of the primitive groove to take up their positions as one of the germ layers. The subset of cells that migrate through the anterior region of the primitive streak, the node, are unique in that these cells give rise to a specialized structure called the **notochord**. The notochord is a transient, rodlike, cellular structure that runs along the anterior-posterior axis of the embryo and lies beneath the developing central nervous system. The cells that make up the notochord release molecular signals that instruct the adjacent cells of the overlying ectoderm to change, or begin to differentiate, into neural ectoderm. The ectodermal cells that are initially induced by the notochord in this manner are called the **neural plate**.

In response to this induction, the cells that make up the neural plate take on a distinctly elongated and columnar appearance. The neural plate subsequently folds inward (Figure 6.2) while the nonneural ectodermal cells on either side of the neural plate move toward the center. These nonneural ectodermal cells from either side of the neural plate continue to converge toward one another until they meet and join. This results in a layer of ectoderm, which overlies a tube formed from the neural plate, folding inward and then being pinched together along the dorsal side. This tube is called the **neural tube**, and it eventually forms the brain and spinal cord, as well as many of the various types of neurons, or nerve cells, that are present in the body. The closure of the neural tube as the overlying ectoderm converges and fuses above it does not occur simultaneously along the entire anterior-posterior axis of the developing embryo. In mammals, including humans, the neural tube initiates its closure at a number of locations along the anterior-posterior axis. From these points where its closure is initiated, the neural tube closes in opposite directions along the anterior-posterior axis until it is entirely enclosed.

This process is similar to pinching a Ziploc sandwich bag along the seal at a number of places and then continuing to seal the rest of the bag from these regions. There are known defects in neural tube closure in humans. The congenital malformation called spina bifida is a birth defect that results from a failure of the neural tube to completely close.

## NEURAL CREST

The process of neurulation, in addition to giving rise to the neural tube and central nervous system, also gives rise to a population of cells known as the **neural crest**. When the neural tube is formed by the pinching together of the ectodermal cells lying on either side of the neural plate, a collection of cells initially link the newly formed neural tube and overlying

(continues on page 58)

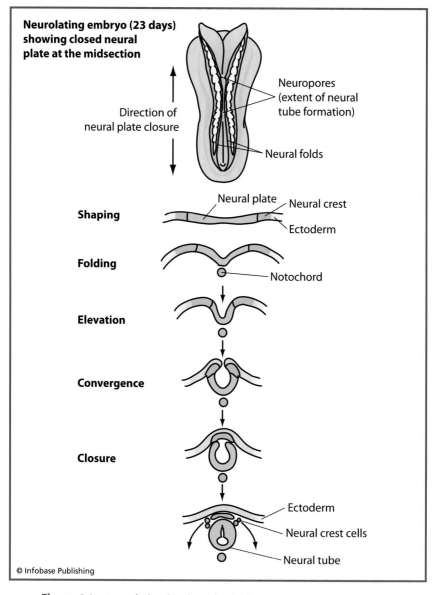

**Neurolating embryo (23 days) showing closed neural plate at the midsection**

Neuropores (extent of neural tube formation)

Direction of neural plate closure

Neural folds

**Shaping**    Neural plate    Neural crest

Ectoderm

**Folding**

Notochord

**Elevation**

**Convergence**

**Closure**

Ectoderm

Neural crest cells

Neural tube

© Infobase Publishing

**Figure 6.2**    Neurulation involves the folding inward and subsequent internalization of surface ectodermal cells. This process of cell movements results in the formation of the neural tube, which gives rise to the central nervous system.

## SPINA BIFIDA

*Spina bifida* (Latin for "divided spine") is one of the most commonly occurring congenital malformations in humans. It is estimated that slightly more than 1 out of 1,000 infants exhibit this birth defect, which involves delayed or improper closure of the neural tube. This defect also leads to abnormalities in the bone, muscle, and skin surrounding the brain and spinal cord. The most common and mildest form of this malformation, spina bifida occulta, results from the failure of a single vertebra to fuse dorsally. The only outwardly visible sign of this is a small tuft of hair or perhaps a small dimple over the affected vertebra. In addition, there is no pain or neurological defect associated with this form. A more severe form of this malformation, spina bifida cystica, is considerably less common. This form results when multiple vertebrae fail to fuse, leading to the spinal cord bulging out into a skin-covered cyst on the outside of the body. This is typically accompanied by neurological disorders whose severity is dependent on the degree to which neural tissue bulges into the cyst.

Severe spina bifida can also accompany the related congenital malformation *anencephaly* (Greek for "not brain"). This malformation is lethal and results in the fetus spontaneously aborting or the infant afflicted with it dying shortly after birth. Anencephaly, like spina bifida, results from the failure of the neural tube to close. Whereas spina bifida involves defects more posteriorly, anencephaly results from defects more anteriorly, specifically in the cephalic or brain region. This failure of the anterior neural tube to close during neurulation leads to the degeneration of the forebrain and the failure of the vault of the skull to form. Interestingly, studies have shown that more than half of the incidences of spina bifida and anencephaly in humans can be prevented by supplementing the diet of pregnant women with folic acid. For this reason, the Centers for Disease Control and Prevention recommends that all women of childbearing age take folic acid daily to reduce the risk of neural tube defects during pregnancy.

*(continued from page 55)*

ectoderm. It is these cells, which lie between the future central nervous system and future epidermis, that become the neural crest. Neural crest cells migrate extensively throughout the body during development and also give rise to a large number of cell types and structures. Interestingly, neural crest cells can give rise to cell types not normally associated with being derived from ectoderm. For example, neural crest cells that appear during the closure of the anterior, or cranial, region of the neural tube give rise to facial cartilage and bone, as well as the smooth muscle of the face, head, and neck. Other derivatives of the neural crest include components of the peripheral nervous system, components of the endocrine and paracrine systems, pigment cells, and even components of the teeth. Because the neural crest plays an important role in the development of all vertebrates, including humans, it is sometimes referred to as the fourth germ layer.

## THE BRAIN

Before neurulation is complete, the anterior region of the neural tube, which will give rise to the brain, is already undergoing significant further development. At approximately four weeks into development, the presumptive brain forms as three bulges in the anterior neural tube. These are the forebrain, or **prosencephalon**; the midbrain, or **mesencephalon**; and the hindbrain, or **rhombencephalon** (Figure 6.3).

The forebrain shortly gives rise to the **optic vesicles**, which extend outward from each side. The forebrain subdivides further into the anterior **telencephalon**, which will become the cerebrum, and the more posterior **diencephalon**, which will give rise to the **thalamus** and **hypothalamus**, the regions of the brain involved in processing sensory impulses and various automatic functions, such as body temperature regulation.

The midbrain gives rise to structures such as the optic lobes and tectum and controls functions that relate to vision and hearing.

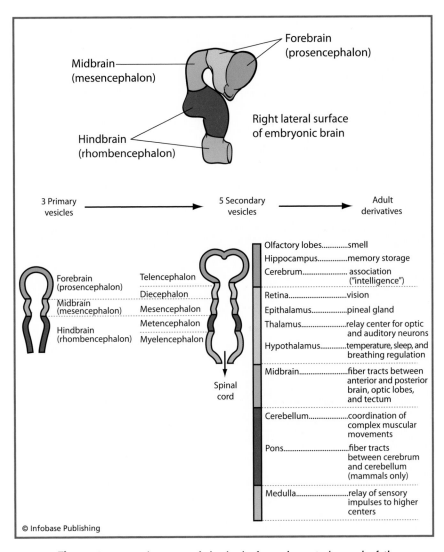

Forebrain
(prosencephalon)

Midbrain
(mesencephalon)

Right lateral surface
of embryonic brain

Hindbrain
(rhombencephalon)

3 Primary
vesicles

5 Secondary
vesicles

Adult
derivatives

Forebrain
(prosencephalon)

Telencephalon

Diencephalon

Midbrain
(mesencephalon)

Mesencephalon

Metencephalon

Hindbrain
(rhombencephalon)

Myelencephalon

Spinal
cord

Olfactory lobes.............smell
Hippocampus...............memory storage
Cerebrum...................... association
                                        ("intelligence")
Retina...............................vision
Epithalamus.................pineal gland
Thalamus......................relay center for optic
                                        and auditory neurons
Hypothalamus.............temperature, sleep, and
                                        breathing regulation
Midbrain........................fiber tracts between
                                        anterior and posterior
                                        brain, optic lobes,
                                        and tectum
Cerebellum...................coordination of
                                        complex muscular
                                        movements
Pons...............................fiber tracts
                                        between cerebrum
                                        and cerebellum
                                        (mammals only)
Medulla........................relay of sensory
                                        impulses to higher
                                        centers

© Infobase Publishing

**Figure 6.3**  Development of the brain from the anterior end of the neural tube is illustrated here. The brain develops from three primary vesicles (the forebrain, midbrain, and hindbrain) that further subdivide into their adult derivatives. The three primary vesicles begin to form about four weeks into development.

The hindbrain will come to control movements of the body as well as the vital automatic functions of the internal organs. Like the forebrain, the hindbrain, or rhombencephalon, subdivides. During its development, the hindbrain takes on a segmental pattern, where each segment is called a **rhombomere**. Each rhombomere represents a separate developmental compartment so cells from one rhombomere cannot mix with cells from another, and each rhombomere has its own distinct developmental fate. The rhombomeres give rise to the cranial nerves, which carry signals from the brain to the muscles, receptors, and glands of the head, neck, and thoracic and abdominal cavities.

## CONNECTIONS

The process of neurulation involves the involution of a region of the dorsal ectoderm, which positions a tube of cells just beneath the dorsal surface of the developing body. This neural tube gives rise to the central nervous system, including the brain and spinal cord. As development proceeds, the posterior neural tube gives rise to the spinal cord. The surrounding mesoderm gives rise to a protective covering of bone in the form of vertebrae. The anterior region of the neural tube develops into the different compartments of the brain that are encased in a skull derived from mesoderm.

# 7

# Establishing the Axes

THE PREVIOUS TWO CHAPTERS HAVE PRIMARILY FOCUSED ON questions of human development concerning morphogenesis and differentiation. These two developmental processes obviously play a very important role in the events associated with gastrulation and neurulation. Morphogenic movements during both of these events rearrange the cells and shape the general body plan of the developing embryo. As cells are being positioned in this manner, they are also beginning to take on more specificity in terms of their form and function. Cells positioned on the inside of the embryo develop according to endodermal and mesodermal pathways, while cells on the surface of the embryo develop into various kinds of ectodermal cells, including epidermis, or skin, cells. Neurulation positions a subset of the ectodermal cells such that they will give rise to the central nervous system, including the brain and spinal cord.

As the embryo undergoes gastrulation, the axes of the body are established. The position of the node of the primitive streak reflects the anterior pole of the anterior-posterior axis of the embryo and, ultimately, the adult. In addition, the surface of the embryonic disc that will migrate through the primitive streak during gastrulation is destined to become the dorsal side of the embryo. Thus, by the time that gastrulation is completed, the anterior-posterior and dorsal-ventral axes are defined.

The early development of the embryonic axes is important because the axes essentially establish and outline a very general layout for the developing body, including which end is anterior and which is posterior, which side is dorsal and which is ventral, and which is left and right. Subsequent developmental events then position specific structures and tissues in relation to these axes. To accomplish this, however, additional information is needed so that specific developmental events and processes occur at the correct location along the established axes. In other words, the regions along the axes must be further refined. For example, before limb development can begin, information must be present to specify the precise position along the anterior-posterior axis of the trunk from which the arm or leg will grow. This positional information is specified along the anterior-posterior axis by a group of genes called the *Hox* **genes.**

## *HOX* GENES PATTERN THE ANTERIOR-POSTERIOR AXIS

The concept that many animals share common elements during their development illustrates the remarkable relatedness among all animals. It is because of this that biologists can study different organisms as model systems to gain a better understanding of human biology. The *Hox* genes are an excellent example of a group of genes that are found in many different kinds of animals and that perform a similar function in these different animals. Studying the functions of *Hox* genes in one animal is, therefore, likely to provide insights into the role of *Hox* genes in another animal.

The *Hox* genes are a group of genes that were first discovered in mutants of the fruit fly *Drosophila melanogaster*. A number of *Drosophila* mutants are classified as being homeotic. A *homeotic mutation* is one where the change in a gene results in the transformation of the identity of one region of an

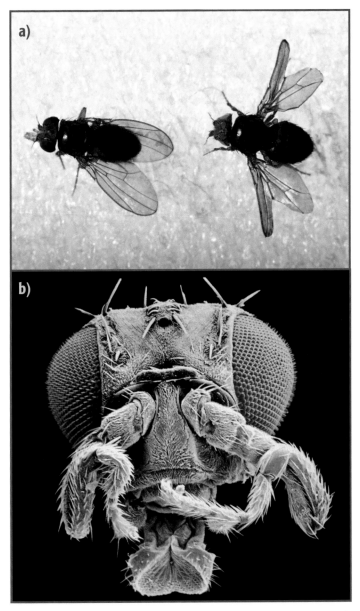

**Figure 7.1**  Certain genes control the formation of certain body parts in an organism. If this gene is mutated, development may be altered. This phenomenon was first observed in the common fruit fly *Drosophila melanogaster*. Seen here are *Drosophila* with the *bithorax* mutation in which the fly grows an extra pair of wings (*top*) and *Drosophila* displaying the *antennapedia* mutatation in which legs replace antennae (*bottom*).

organism into the identity of another region, an effect called *homeosis*. Two such *Drosophila* mutants are the *bithorax* and *antennapedia* mutant flies (Figure 7.1). In the *bithorax* mutant fly, the third thoracic segment takes on the second thoracic segment's identity and grows an extra set of wings. Thus, this mutation results in a fly with two sets of wings rather than one. Similarly, in the *antennapedia* mutant, a region of the fly's head has taken on the identity of the fly's thorax and sprouts legs rather than antennae.

If these mutant flies are considered from a patterning point of view, they exhibit the transformation of the identity of one

## MUTATIONS

Mutations result from alterations in the nucleotide sequence of the genome. Mutations can arise anywhere along a chromosome including in the coding region of a gene or in regulatory regions that direct the expression of a gene. Chapter 3 introduced the concept that the nucleotide sequence of DNA represents the blueprints that direct the actions and functions of a cell and, by extension, the organism made up of such cells. Changes, or mutations, in the nucleotide sequence alter these blueprints, thus also altering cellular processes. The effects of mutations on the organism can vary. A mutation can have absolutely no effect on the organism, or it can have a significant impact. For example, a single nucleotide change in the human hemoglobin gene is the cause of sickle cell disease. In addition, mutations in genes that control cell division can often lead to cancer. Mutations can also alter the outward appearance of an organism. For example, mutations in the human fibroblast growth factor receptor *FGFR1* gene causes Pfeiffer syndrome, which is characterized by limb defects and abnormalities in the shape of the face and skull.

Mutations can be incredibly valuable tools with which to study developmental biology. If a mutant gene leads to a developmental defect or an alteration in the appearance of an organism, identifying

region into the identity of another region. This transformation involves alterations in the positional information along the anterior-posterior axis. In the *bithorax* mutant, for example, the third thoracic segment takes on the identity of a more anterior segment, and in the *antennapedia* mutant, a region of the head takes on the identity of a more posterior region. This suggests that the mutant genes in these homeotic flies likely play some role in patterning the anterior-posterior axis.

There are actually nine different *Hox* genes in the *Drosophila* genome, and each one is named for the homeotic phenotype that results when that gene is mutated. Interestingly, genes are

that gene can provide insight into the normal function of the wild type, or non-mutated, gene. Consider Pfeiffer syndrome, for example. The identification of the gene that, when mutated, leads to the malformations associated with this syndrome will also identify a gene that is likely involved in limb and cranio-facial development. Model organisms are often manipulated experimentally to mutate specific genes so that the effect of these mutations, and therefore the role of the genes, can be examined. The 2007 Nobel Prize in Physiology or Medicine was awarded to scientists who developed a technique that causes mutations in specific genes in mice so that their functions can be studied. Some model organisms, such as *Drosophila* and zebrafish, have been subjected to mutagenetic screens, and work is currently being done to perform a screen in the mouse model system as well. In experiments of this type, the organisms are treated to induce random mutations, which often results in organisms with developmental defects. By determining the genes that have been mutated, biologists can then implicate those genes in the normal development of the region of the organism carrying the defect. The 1995 Nobel Prize in Physiology or Medicine that was awarded to scientists, in part, for performing the mutagenic screen in *Drosophila*, highlights the importance of this type of science.

typically clustered in the genome as is shown in Figure 7.2. Within this cluster of genes, their order along the chromosome reflects the effects of the mutations on the anterior-posterior axis of the fly. Thus, mutations in the left-most (3') genes in the cluster affect the most anterior body parts, and mutations in the right-most (5') genes in the cluster affect more posterior regions of the fly. The expression patterns of these genes during *Drosophila* development is such that they are expressed spatially and temporally in the order in which they sit in their clusters. Genes at the 3' end of the cluster are expressed first and more anteriorly in the developing embryo than the genes at the other end of the cluster (Figure 7.2).

Vertebrates, including humans, also have versions, or homologues, of these homeotic genes. In fact, it appears that all animals not only have homologues of these genes, but that the genomic organization and function of these genes is also incredibly well conserved in all animals. Humans and other vertebrates have many more *Hox* genes than *Drosophila*. Rather than having one cluster of nine genes, as in *Drosophila*, humans have four clusters consisting of as many as thirteen genes. Also, rather than having names such as *antennapedia* or *ultrabithorax,* the vertebrate *Hox* genes are named using a series of letters and numbers. Each of the four clusters is identified by a letter, so they are called the *Hoxa, Hoxb, Hoxc,* and *Hoxd* clusters. Each gene is also assigned a number to reflect its position relative to the thirteen possible places it can occupy in a particular cluster. For example, the most 3' (or left-most) gene in the *Hoxa* cluster is *Hoxa1*, while the gene at the opposite end of the cluster is *Hoxa13*.

In vertebrates, the expression pattern of the *Hox* genes along the anterior-posterior axis of the developing embryo is consistent with that already described for *Drosophila* and is schematized at the bottom of Figure 7.2 (mouse embryo). Genes at the 3' end of the cluster are expressed first and more anteriorly (e.g., the hindbrain) than genes more 5' in the cluster, which are expressed more posteriorly. In addition, mutations

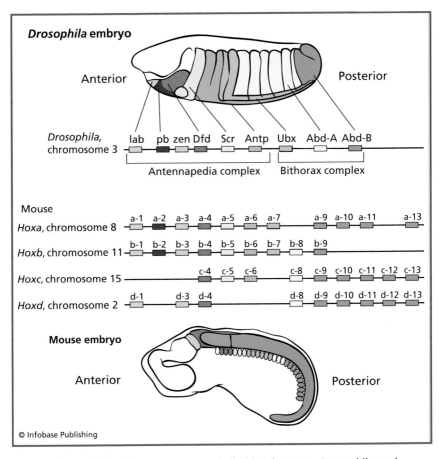

**Figure 7.2** There are many similarities between *Drosophila* and mammalian *Hox* genes in terms of their organization in the genome and expression during development. Homology between genes is represented by use of the same colors and approximate regions of expression of these genes in the embryos.

in the *Hox* clusters are able to produce homeotic phenotypes similar in nature to those observed in *Drosophila*, although the phenotypes are generally less spectacular and more subtle. For example, mice that have had their *Hoxc-8* gene mutated exhibit an extra fourteenth pair of ribs on the first lumbar vertebra, which normally do not have ribs. Such homeotic transformations that can be directly attributed to mutations in *Hox* genes have not been described in humans to date, although human *Hox* mutations have been described as leading to other developmental defects as well as cancer. The organization, number, and the expression of human *Hox* genes is consistent with their expression in the mouse and there is little doubt that these genes are playing the same role in humans as they do in virtually every other animal.

The *Hox* genes code for the production of proteins that act as transcription factors, and the role they play in anterior-posterior patterning is through the regulation of other genes. The concept of transcription was previously introduced as the first step in decoding the information in the gene to produce a protein. Transcription factors, such as Hox proteins, essentially control when and where other genes are activated or inactivated. Also in Chapter 3, it was mentioned that, in general, not all of the 20,000 to 25,000 or so genes that make up the human genome are active in the same cells at the same time. It is because of this differential gene expression that cells can differ in their appearance and function. The factors that control which genes are active and inactive in a given cell or in a given region of the developing embryo play an incredibly important role—the products of the *Hox* genes that act as regulators or molecular switches and control gene activity.

Essentially, the *Hox* genes function by being expressed differentially in different regions of the developing embryo. The Hox proteins that these genes code for act as regional control switches that can direct the developmental future of a region of the embryo. They accomplish this by controlling the activity of specific genes in different regions. For example, in the *Drosophila antennapedia* mutant, the *antennapedia* gene, which is normally expressed in the developing abdomen of the fly, becomes active in a region of the head of the developing fly as well. Under normal circumstances, in the developing abdomen, this gene codes for the production of the antennapedia protein. This protein then regulates the expression of other genes that confer the identity upon this region of the fly, including the genes required to make legs. When the antennapedia protein is produced in the developing head of the fly as a result of a mutation, it performs this same function and regulates the genes required to make legs rather than those genes that would be required to make antennae.

## CONNECTIONS

This chapter has examined how the embryonic axes are established and patterned during development. Initially, patterning comes in the form of broadly establishing the anterior-posterior, dorsal-ventral, and left-right axes of the developing embryo. Positional information along the anterior-posterior axis is further refined through the expression and action of the *Hox* genes. The action mechanism of *Hox* genes and their protein products is conserved, or similar, in virtually all animals, including humans. The *Hox* genes are expressed in specific regions of the embryo, and their protein products are positioned in those same specific regions. The Hox proteins are then able to act as molecular switches that regulate the subsequent expression of other genes that are, in turn, required to code for the production of all the components of the body associated with that particular region. In *Drosophila*, the action of the homeotic genes could be in the form of regulating genes that code for the production of legs or wings. In vertebrates, the action of the *Hox* genes could result in the regulation of genes that code for the production of specific vertebrae, ribs, or limbs.

# 8

# Limb Development

THE PREVIOUS CHAPTERS HAVE FOCUSED ON THE EVENTS THAT generate the external and internal layout of the body. This chapter will focus on the development of organs, a process called **organogenesis**. An organ is a part of a body that is formed from two or more types of tissues and that carries out a specific function. Examples of organs include the eyes, the heart, and the limbs. The primary focus of this chapter will be on limb development because this area of development is fairly well understood. In addition, the developing limb perfectly illustrates the importance of two different tissues interacting with one another as a developmental mechanism.

## THE LIMB BUD

The first morphological indication of limb development is the formation of the limb buds along the trunk of the body. Limb buds form where the arms and legs will develop. Most of the mechanisms that give rise to a leg or an arm, once their identity has been specified, are similar if not identical. Limb buds first typically appear during the fourth week of human development when specialized cells migrate from the mesoderm adjacent to where the future limbs will be located into

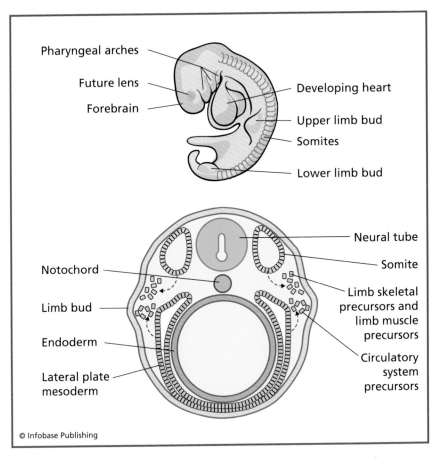

**Figure 8.1**  A schematic diagram of a four-week-old human embryo in profile (*top*) and cross section (*bottom*) is shown here. At this stage, the neural tube is forming, somites are present, and the limb buds have appeared. In the cross section, the limb bud can be seen to be populated by both mesenchyme that has migrated from the somites and by lateral plate mesoderm.

what will become the limb bud (Figure 8.1). These migrating cells originate from two different regions of the mesoderm that make up the trunk of the body: the **somites** and the lateral plate mesoderm.

The somites are compartments of mesoderm located on either side of the neural tube and notochord in the trunk of the embryo. The compartments of somitic mesoderm confer a segmental appearance along the anterior-posterior axis. Each segment represents a distinct population of cells that are generally considered as remaining within a particular somite once they are compartmentalized. Mesodermal cells from the somites give rise to the vertebrae and ribs, which retain the obvious segmental appearance of the somites from which they developed, as well as the skeletal muscle of the back, the trunk of the body, and the limbs. The other region of trunk mesoderm that contributes to the developing limb is known as the *lateral plate mesoderm*. The lateral plate mesoderm lies more ventrally in the trunk, relative to the dorsal somites. The lateral plate mesodermal cells give rise to components of the circulatory system, including the heart, blood vessels, and blood, in addition to giving rise to all of the mesodermal components of the limb other than the somite-derived musculature.

The specialized cells that are released from the trunk mesoderm to begin limb development are called **mesenchyme**. These cells have the ability to migrate and to actively divide. When limb development is initiated, these mesenchymal cells migrate laterally, eventually accumulating under the ectodermal tissue of the trunk where they form the mesodermal component of the limb bud. The limb mesenchymal cells at the distal (far) edge of the limb bud induce a change in the ectoderm that overlies them to become the ectodermal component of the limb bud. This general mechanism of two different tissues, in this case mesoderm and ectoderm, interacting with each other is similar in principle to neural induction where the notochord releases factors to initiate the formation of the neural plate. In this case, the signal released by the limb mesenchyme induces the overlying ectodermal cells to elongate. The factor that is released by the limb bud mesenchyme is a protein called *fibroblast growth factor 10* (FGF10).

When FGF10 is released by the mesenchymal cells, it makes its way to the adjacent layer of ectodermal cells where it signals these cells to elongate. The elongated cells form a thickened structure, called the *apical ectodermal ridge* (AER), which runs along the distal edge of the limb bud. The AER is crucial for limb development because it acts as a signaling center. In much the same way that the mesenchyme of the limb bud induces formation of the AER, the cells of the AER, in turn, produce factors that make their way to the adjacent mesenchymal cells where they act as signals that instruct these cells how to act.

One of the factors released by the AER is the *protein fibroblast growth factor 8* (FGF8). These AER-produced growth factors instruct the adjacent, underlying mesenchyme, a region known as the **progress zone** (Figure 8.2), to continue its growth. The limb grows along a proximal-distal axis where the proximal (near) end of the axis is the trunk of the body and the distal end is the region of growth that culminates with the formation of digits. Experiments performed in chick embryos beautifully illustrate the importance of the AER. The removal of the AER from embryonic chick limbs causes limb development to stop at that particular stage, resulting in

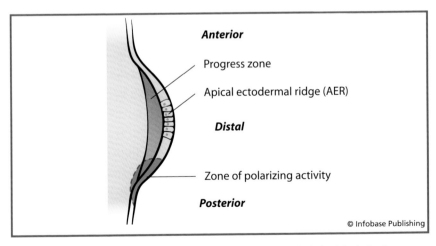

**Figure 8.2**   Important regions of the developing limb bud include the progress zone, the zone of polarizing activity (zone of polarizing activity, or ZPA), and the apical ectodermal ridge (AER).

a truncated limb (Figure 8.3). The removal of the AER early in development results in a severely truncated limb, while its later removal results in a more complete limb. In essence, what is occurring in these studies is that the removal of the AER also removes the signal, or signals, for the limb bud to continue its development.

Together, the AER and progress zone lead to the outgrowth along the proximal-distal axis of the developing limb through their communication with each other via released growth factors. In a very general sense, it might be considered, then, that the AER is specifying the distal, or far, end of this axis. Limbs are typically polar structures in terms of the anterior-posterior and dorsal-ventral axes, as well as the proximal-distal axis. This means that each end of each axis of the limb, beyond the proximity to the trunk of the body, is different, whether considering the organization of fingers and toes or the surfaces of a hand or foot, for example. Additional mechanisms must therefore exist to pattern this polarity. The anterior-posterior axis of the limb relates to the organization of digits. The anterior end of this axis corresponds to the future location of the thumb, and the posterior end corresponds to the future location of the pinky finger.

Positional information along the anterior-posterior axis initially originates from a region localized at the posterior margin of the limb bud, which is called the **zone of polarizing activity (ZPA)**. The cells of the ZPA provide this positional information by producing and releasing a factor that informs cells in the vicinity that they are in the posterior region of the developing limb. The factor produced by the cells of the ZPA is a protein called Sonic hedgehog (Shh). The importance of Shh acting as the polarizing signal that defines the posterior region of the limb bud can be illustrated in experiments in chick embryos. These experiments are similar to those described for elucidating the importance of the AER. The addition of ectopic Shh protein to the anterior side of the limb bud, the region opposite that of the ZPA, leads to a mirror image duplication

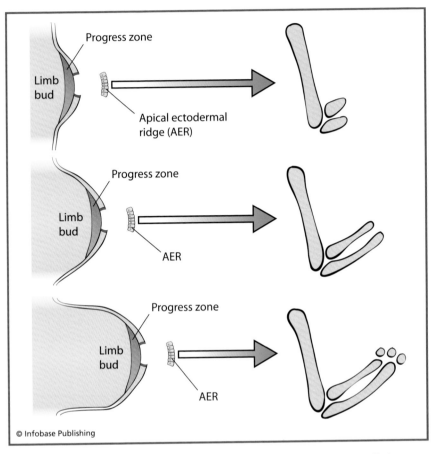

**Figure 8.3** Removal of the apical ectodermal ridge (AER) causes limb development to cease at that particular stage and ultimately results in a truncated limb. The degree of truncation depends on how early in development the AER was removed. This diagram shows three examples of three different stages of development.

of digits (Figure 8.4). This indicates that Shh is able to induce cells that normally have an anterior identity into cells that have a posterior identity. This essentially disrupts the anterior-posterior axis of the limb bud, such that each end of this axis takes on a posterior identity instead of one end having posterior identity and the other anterior identity.

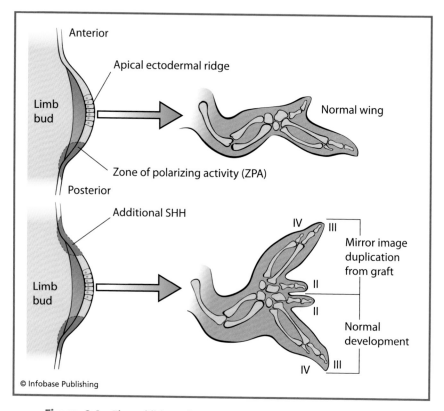

**Figure 8.4** The addition of ectopic sonic hedgehog (Shh) to the anterior side of the limb bud leads to a mirror image duplication of digits in experiments in chicks (shown in the bottom diagram). The top diagram represents normal development. This finding suggests that Shh can functionally substitute for the zone of polarizing activity.

The mechanism for specifying the remaining dorsal-ventral axis of the limb, where the dorsal region will eventually develop nails and the ventral region will develop into the palm or sole, is similar to what has already been discussed. The dorsal ectoderm of the limb bud produces a protein called *Wnt7a*. This protein then induces the adjacent dorsal mesenchyme to activate a gene called *Lmx1*. Like the *Hox* genes, *Lmx1* codes for the production of a transcription factor, and the product of this gene, the Lmx1 protein, is able to regulate additional genes in the dorsal mesenchyme that provide instructions for the formation of dorsal structures. In fact, nail-patella syndrome is characterized by a lack of dorsal structures, including nails and kneecaps, and is found in humans who lack functional *LMX1* genes.

The initial establishment of the axes of the limb bud can be seen to be, in part, a result of the interplay between the ectoderm and mesoderm layers that make up that bud. In general, the importance of factors that can either diffuse to other cells (as in the case of the AER) or that can define regions of the limb bud (as in the case of the ZPA) to induce a response is clear. This general establishment of the axes defines directionality in the limb bud; however, additional factors further refine the pattern of the limb. Much as the anterior-posterior axis of the embryonic trunk is first established and then further refined by the action of the *Hox* genes, so the developing limb is first patterned broadly, by the mechanisms described above, and then refined further by the action of those same *Hox* genes.

If one considers the limbs of a human, a distinct pattern can be observed that is conserved between arms and legs, particularly at the skeletal level (Figure 8.5). Along the proximal-distal axis, both upper arms and legs contain a single bone, the humerus and femur, respectively, that are the most proximal structures. This region of the limb is sometimes referred to as the **stylopod**. The region of the limb adjacent and distal to this bone, sometimes called the **zeugopod**, contains the ulna and radius in the forearm and the tibia and fibula in the lower leg. Finally, adjacent and distal to this region is the **autopod**, which is made up of the wrist, hand, and fingers, or ankle, foot, and toes. The pattern of a human limb from the proximal to distal end is thus made up of at least three distinct segments: the stylopod, zeugopod, and autopod. These limbs develop in stages from the proximal to

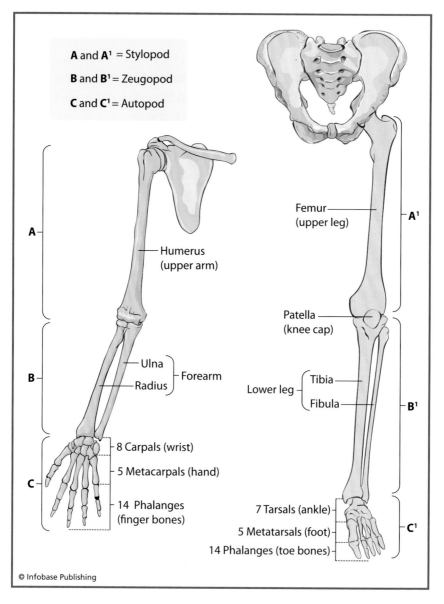

A and A¹ = Stylopod

B and B¹ = Zeugopod

C and C¹ = Autopod

A

Humerus
(upper arm)

Femur
(upper leg) — A¹

Patella
(knee cap)

B

Ulna
Radius
Forearm

Tibia
Fibula
Lower leg

B¹

8 Carpals (wrist)

5 Metacarpals (hand)

C

14 Phalanges
(finger bones)

7 Tarsals (ankle)

5 Metatarsals (foot)

14 Phalanges (toe bones)

C¹

© Infobase Publishing

**Figure 8.5**   A distinct and conserved pattern can be observed between arms and legs, particularly at the skeletal level. For example, the humerus and femur are similar in nature, as are the bones of the forearm and lower leg and the phalanges that make up the toes and fingers.

the distal such that the stylopod develops first followed by the zeugopod and autopod.

During limb development, the *Hox* genes are expressed in the limb bud in a manner consistent with that observed in the trunk of the body. One major difference is that not all of the *Hox* genes are expressed. It appears that group 9 to group 13 genes are the major ones involved in limb patterning. In addition, it seems that two of the *Hox* clusters are predominantly involved in general limb patterning, with genes found in the other two playing more restricted and specific roles. The *Hoxd* cluster is typically associated with limb development, as is the *Hoxa* cluster to a certain extent. The *Hoxb* and *Hoxc* clusters are active to lesser extents and appear to play roles in either forelimb or hind limb development. Each of the three segments of the developing limb exhibits a particular signature of expression of *Hox* genes. Specific *Hox* genes are expressed during development of the stylopod, a different complement of *Hox* genes is expressed in the developing zeugopod, and still another complement is expressed during autopod development. Just as the disruption of *Hox* gene expression during development of the trunk can have a serious impact on its appearance, so can disruption of *Hox* expression impact the appearance of the limb. For example, mice that do not have the functional *Hoxa-11* and *Hoxd-11* genes completely lack the ulna and radius of their forelimbs.

## DIGIT PATTERNING

Interestingly, the *Hox* genes pattern the anterior-posterior axis of the limb as well as the proximal-distal axis. The pattern of the limb along the anterior-posterior axis is slightly more obvious, particularly the order of the fingers and toes. As mentioned previously, the thumb (or big toe) represents the anterior end of the axis and the pinky finger (or little toe) represents the posterior end. As has been observed for the expression along the anterior-posterior axis of the trunk and along the proximal-distal axis of the limb, regions of the developing autopod are also characterized along the ante-

## A HUMAN *HOX* MUTATION

Recently, the first human malformations resulting from the disruption of the action of a *Hox* gene have been described. One such malformation relates to limb development. Human synpolydactyly syndrome (Figure 8.6) is outwardly characterized by the fusion of digits, the fingers, and toes. (*Polydactyly* means having more than the normal number of fingers or toes.) This syndrome results from mutations in the *Hoxd-13* gene. Based on what has been observed in other animals, mutations in *Hox* genes could be expected to give rise to homeotic mutations, where one region of the body takes on the identity of another. However, the outward appearance of the hands and feet of people who suffer from synpolydactyly syndrome are not necessarily consistent with what might be predicted to be associated with a mutation in a *Hox* gene. Closer examination of the hands and feet of people with this syndrome, however, reveals that this syndrome actually is consistent with a homeosis. X-ray analysis of the hands and feet of people suffering from synpolydactyly syndrome reveal the transformation of the bones of the hand into ones that more resemble the bones of the wrist (the metacarpals are transformed into carpals) and the transformation of the bones of the foot into ones that more closely resemble those of the ankle (the metatarsals are transformed into tarsals). These transformations truly are homeotic in nature and represent a region of the limb taking on the identity of another region. This is very much like, in principal, what is seen in other animals whose *Hox* genes have been mutated: mice carrying a

rior-posterior axis by specific signatures of *Hox* gene expression. Transformations in identity of the components of the anterior-posterior axis of the limb have also been characterized in association with disruptions in *Hox* gene function.

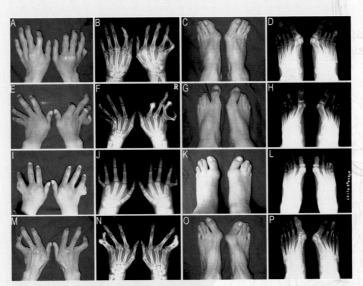

**Figure 8.6** A mutation in the human *Hoxd-13* gene can result in limb malformation. Photographs and X-rays showing hand and foot malformations as a result of this mutation are shown here. Notice the partial fusion of the fingers and toes.

mutation in the *Hoxc-8* gene have an extra fourteenth pair of ribs on the first lumbar vertebra, which normally do not have ribs, or the *bithorax* mutant *Drosophila*, where one or more segments of the fly takes on the identity of another and develops wings rather than halteres.

## CONNECTIONS

The developing limb is a complex process that is dependent on many simultaneously occurring mechanisms. Outgrowth of the limb from the trunk of the body along the proximal-distal axis is dependent on the interaction between the AER and progress zone. Because organs are generally formed from multiple tissues, the interaction between ectoderm (the AER) and mesoderm (the progress zone) is an excellent model that can be used to understand organogenesis. As is observed during patterning of the trunk, early patterning of the limb involves broadly establishing the axes (for example, the signals released by the ZPA) and then refining these axes. In fact, this chapter has illustrated how many of the mechanisms that are used during development of the trunk of the body can be used again, in a different context, to control additional aspects of development, in this case, the limbs. For example, the *Hox* genes not only have a role in the specification of where limbs form, they also play a role in the patterning of the anterior-posterior and proximal-distal axes of the limb. This is actually a common theme in developmental biology, where mechanisms may be used in different contexts and at different times to accomplish similar functions. Interestingly, many of these mechanisms are also well conserved between different animals. In the context of limb development, for example, the genes and their expression and function that have been described here in relation to human development are also found animals as diverse as mice and birds, and to a certain extent, even fish. It is for this reason that development can provide many insights into what makes organisms similar and what makes them different.

# 9

# The Delicate Embryo

THE PURPOSE OF THIS BOOK HAS BEEN TO HIGHLIGHT SOME OF the major and better-understood developmental processes by which a single cell becomes an embryo, a fetus, and ultimately a baby. It is hoped that the reader has some appreciation for how delicate and finely balanced many of these processes are. Genes must be activated or repressed in the proper cells with the correct timing, and cells must communicate via the proper concentration of released factors. For development to proceed, there is often very little room for error. Evidence to support this comes in many forms, the most obvious being how easily development can be disrupted. Spina bifida, as described in Chapter 6, is a birth defect caused by a disruption of the developmental process of neurulation. Mutations such as those to the *FGFR1* gene, described in Chapter 7, or *Hox* genes, as described in Chapter 8, have also been shown to cause birth defects.

It is estimated that approximately 3% of human infants are born in the United States with some kind of observable physical abnormality. Examples of some of the more common birth defects include heart defects, cleft palate, cleft lip, spina bifida, missing limbs, and missing or additional fingers and/or toes

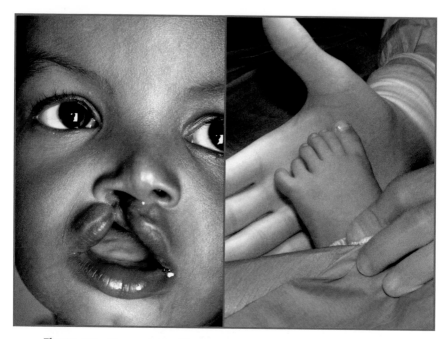

**Figure 9.1** These photos illustrate some examples of human birth defects. In the left photograph, a young boy has a cleft lip, characterized by the opening in the upper lip between the mouth and nose. The right photo shows a child with polydactyly (the presence of extra fingers or toes). In this case, the child was born with six toes on each foot instead of five.

(Figure 9.1). In addition, it is estimated that as many as 70% of pregnancies result in a miscarriage. The majority of these spontaneous abortions, or miscarriages, are thought to be caused by chromosomal abnormalities, but more than half of the physical abnormalities found at birth are due to unknown causes. Several factors are known to cause birth defects, however. The genetic makeup of the developing embryo affects many of the developmental processes. Just as the developing embryo inherits the instructions for its future hair and eye color from its parents, it is also possible for the embryo to inherit information that has been changed or mutated, which can potentially lead to some kind of abnormality or even to its termination. It is for this reason that it is not unusual for an infant to exhibit the same birth defect as a parent. The conditions, or environment, in which the embryo develops also play a role. During the past several decades, it has become relatively common knowledge that substances taken in by a pregnant woman can potentially have serious consequences on the developing embryo. Pregnant women are advised to monitor their nutritional intake and to take supplements, such as folic aid, when necessary. They are also advised not to smoke or drink alcohol so as not to harm the child they carry. Many over-the-counter and prescription medications are also potentially harmful to a developing human, and many of these medications carry warning labels that they should not be used by pregnant women for this very reason. Embryonic development is incredibly sensitive and outside agents can alter normal developmental events even at very low doses. Chemicals and other factors that can disrupt development and lead to birth defects are called **teratogens** (Greek word for "monster formers"). These substances can include: the aforementioned alcohol, cigarettes, and medications; environmental agents, such as pesticides, lead, and organic solvents; diseases, such as chickenpox, measles and genital herpes; and radiation. Although the mechanisms by which some teratogens can affect normal development are understood, others are not.

The most common birth defects are those that affect the heart; it is estimated that 1% of all babies born exhibit a heart defect. Heart defects are actually made up of a number of different types of imperfections and, in general, are considered to include obstructions or blockages, which affect the flow of blood through the heart or the large vessels in its vicinity. They can also affect the actual development of components of the heart. Heart defects are known to have genetic causes such as chromosomal abnormalities and various other mutations, as well as by maternal infections and illnesses, such as measles and diabetes, during pregnancy. The consumption

(continues on page 88)

## THE TERATOGEN THALIDOMIDE

During the early to mid-1950s, a drug company in Germany developed the drug called thalidomide, which caused test subjects to go into a very deep sleep. Scientists working for this company also found that they could treat laboratory animals with extremely high doses of thalidomide had virtually no effects on laboratory animals. Because of this, thalidomide was declared to be nontoxic and therefore very safe. This drug was very quickly released into the marketplace where, alone or in combination with other drugs, it was sold and utilized as a completely safe remedy for ailments such as the flu, colds, headaches, anxiety, and, of course, sleeplessness. Thalidomide was marketed under a number of different brand names and eventually expanded into international markets, ultimately becoming available in close to fifty countries throughout Europe, Asia, Africa, and the Americas. Its biggest selling point was its complete safety; it was considered to be impossible to take a toxic dose. Because of this apparent safety, thalidomide was eventually prescribed to pregnant women who were suffering from morning sickness, nervousness, or insomnia. In fact, the company that developed thalidomide, as well as its distributors, declared it to be the best and safest drug for pregnant women.

Within a year of thalidomide becoming available to the general public, medical doctors began noticing an increase in the number of babies born with **phocomelia**. Phocomelia is characterized by the hands and feet of the child being attached to abbreviated, or shortened, arms and legs (Figure 9.2). In extreme cases, the limbs were completely absent with the hands and feet attached directly to the trunk of the body. The physical appearance associated with phocomelia is the basis for its name, which combines *phoco-* (Greek "seal") and *melia* (Greek "limb") to describe the deformed limb's similarity to the flippers of a seal. Phocomelia is an extremely rare birth defect, estimated to occur once in approximately four million births. In fact, the usual incidence of phocomelia is so low that it is likely that most physicians would never observe a case of it during their entire careers. Thus, it was with great surprise that physicians began to see a number of such cases or became aware of several such births occurring within a certain region within a very short time span. To determine the cause of this epidemic, comparisons were made in an attempt to discover some common element shared by the mothers who carried and gave birth to these deformed infants. The one common element in these births was that the mothers all used medication that contained thalidomide during their pregnancy.

Thalidomide was available to the general public for approximately four years

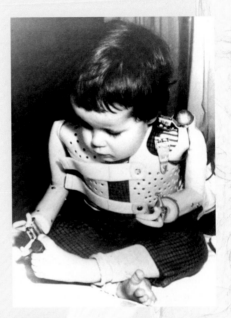

**Figure 9.2** This child was born with birth defects resulting from the use of the teratogen thalidomide by the mother during the pregnancy. Due to the drug's effects on development, the child is lacking hands and arms.

(1957–1961). It is estimated that during that time 8,000 to 12,000 babies were born with birth defects as a direct result of their mothers using medications that contained thalidomide. Less than half of these children survived past their childhood. Furthermore, as little as one dose of thalidomide, taken during preganancy, was found to be sufficient to induce birth defects. These statistics do not take into account the number of children born with internal damage caused by thalidomide, nor do they take into account the number of pregnancies that did not come to term as a result of the damage to the embryo caused by the drug. Conservative estimates, taking these

(continues on page 88)

(continued from page 87)
additional factors into consideration, triple the number of pregnancies affected by thalidomide. The exact mechanism by which
thalidomide actually acts to disrupt development is still a mystery.
One hypothesis is that thalidomide inhibits the growth of the limb
bud mesenchyme. The inhibition or disruption of the progress zone
could potentially lead to phocomelia or the loss of proximal limb
structures such as the stylopod and/or zeugopod that characterizes
birth defects resulting from exposure to thalidomide. Disruptions in
*Hox* patterning along the proximal-distal axis of the limb could also
result in this type of malformation. The loss of the ulna and radius,
or zeugopod, in the forelimbs of mice that are lacking the functional
*Hoxa-11* and *Hoxd-11* genes supports this hypothesis.

(continued from page 85)

of drugs, including alcohol, are also known to lead to these
types of defects. Another common birth defect affects cranio-facial development and is manifested as cleft lip and/or
palate. Clefting arises when tissues of the developing head
fail to fuse properly together, leaving a gap. Cleft lip appears
as a slit, or opening in the top lip that extends to the base of
the nose. Cleft palate is an opening in the roof of the mouth
that results in the mouth being connected to the nasal cavity.
Like heart defects, clefting can be caused by genetic factors
as well as by environmental effects such as smoking, drugs,
and alcohol. These birth defects are often correctable with
reconstructive surgery.

The brief description of heart and oral birth defects has
illustrated how genetic and environmental factors can have a
negative impact on embryonic development. In both cases, the
role of alcohol was described as contributing to these defects.
There is absolutely no doubt that pregnant women should
avoid the consumption of alcohol. Alcohol use by a mother

during pregnancy has clearly been associated with a number of birth defects and fetal alcohol syndrome (FAS). FAS encompasses a number of permanent birth defects that primarily affect the central nervous system as well as fetal growth and facial development. Babies born with FAS are typically below average in height and weight and often exhibit facial features such as small eye openings and thin upper lips. The effects on the central nervous system and brain development can lead to deficits in attention and memory and are also thought to lead to problems later in life, including drug addiction and mental health problems. FAS is also the leading cause of mental retardation in the United States.

## CONNECTIONS

Human development begins with the fertilization of an egg by a sperm. During the span of 264 days, this first cell gives rise to many cells that undergo changes at the molecular and cellular levels as they continue to divide and to take on specific fates. This collection of cells eventually takes on form and, as gastrulation occurs, the cells begin to position themselves to reflect the eventual role in the embryo. Axes form that define the front and back, left and right, and top and bottom of the developing embryo. The nervous system forms as do organs, and throughout this entire process, the embryo and then the fetus continue to grow. This book has touched upon only a small number of the many events that take place at the cellular, molecular, and genetic levels that control development. Based on these few highlights, however, there is little doubt that the developmental process by which a single cell becomes an embryo and ultimately an adult organism is finely balanced. The large number of defects caused by disruptions of single elements of many of the developmental pathways clearly indicates how delicate and

*(continues)*

*(continued)*

sensitive the developing embryo is. The story of thalidomide is heartbreaking and tragic, but clearly illustrates that a woman must exercise caution during pregnancy. Thalidomide was considered to be very safe and yet it had a very unexpected and horrible underside. Cautions against other agents, such as alcohol, cigarettes, and certain medications, that are also known to cause birth defects, should be taken very seriously. The delicate nature of human development is truly inspiring due to the vast number of events and pathways that occur at the cellular, molecular, and genetic levels and that coordinate to produce every multicellular organism.

# Appendix: Conversion Chart

| Unit (metric) | | Metric to English | | English to Metric | |
|---|---|---|---|---|---|
| **LENGTH** | | | | | |
| Kilometer | km | 1 km | 0.62 mile (mi) | 1 mile (mi) | 1.609 km |
| Meter | m | 1 m | 3.28 feet (ft) | 1 foot (ft) | 0.305 m |
| Centimeter | cm | 1 cm | 0.394 inches (in) | 1 inch (in) | 2.54 cm |
| Millimeter | mm | 1 mm | 0.039 inches (in) | 1 inch (in) | 25.4 mm |
| Micrometer | μm | 1 - millionth of a meter | | | |
| **WEIGHT (MASS)** | | | | | |
| Kilogram | kg | 1 kg | 2.2 pounds (lbs) | 1 pound (lbs) | 0.454 kg |
| Gram | g | 1 g | 0.035 ounces (oz) | 1 ounce (oz) | 28.35 g |
| Milligram | mg | 1 mg | 0.000035 ounces (oz) | | |
| Microgram | μg | 1 - millionth of a gram | | | |
| **VOLUME** | | | | | |
| Liter | L | 1 L | 1.06 quarts | 1 gallon (gal) | 3.785 L |
| | | | | 1 quart (qt) | 0.94 L |
| | | | | 1 pint (pt) | 0.47 L |
| Milliliter | mL or cc | 1 mL | 0.034 fluid ounce (fl oz) | 1 fluid ounce (fl oz) | 29.57 mL |
| Microliter | μL | 1 - millionth of a liter | | | |
| **TEMPERATURE** | | | | | |
| | | $°F = 9/5°C + 32$ | | $°C = 5/9 (°F - 32)$ | |

# Glossary

**Acrosome**   The structure at the tip of the sperm head.

**Activated carrier**   A molecule that contains a particular chemical group connected by a high energy bond. It can donate the energy released by the breaking of this bond to many biochemical reactions.

**Adenosine triphosphate (ATP)**   An energy-storage compound for the cell; adenosine is also a building block of DNA and RNA.

**Amino acid**   One of 20 nitrogen-containing compounds that are the building blocks of proteins.

**Autopod**   The most distal region of the limbs—the wrist, hand, and fingers, or the ankle, foot, and toes.

**Blastocoel**   The hollow cavity inside the blastocyst.

**Blastocyst**   A hollow ball of cells, making up the preembryo, that develops from the morula.

**Chorion**   The outermost layer of cells surrounding the implanted embryo.

**Chromosomes**   The self-replicating structures found in the cell nucleus that carry the hereditary information; composed of DNA and protein.

**Cleavage**   Following fertilization, a rapid series of cell divisions that occurs without growth, thereby reducing the size of the cells.

**Cytoskeleton**   A network of tubular and filamentous proteins that form a scaffolding that acts as a support for the cell and gives it shape; it also is involved in cell movement and in the movement of molecules within the cell.

**Deoxyribonucleic acid**   See DNA.

**Diencephalon**   The posterior region of the forebrain.

**Differentiation**   The process in which cells become specialized in structure and function.

**Diploid cell**   A cell that contains two sets of chromosomes.

**DNA (Deoxyribonucleic acid)**   The nucleic acid that contains the hereditary information; it is found in the cell nucleus and is made up of adenine, cytosine, guanine, and thymine nucleotides.

**Ectoderm**   The outermost germ layer, which gives rise to the skin and central nervous system.

**Embryo**   A developing human from the beginning of week three to the end of week eight.

**Embryonic disc**   The band of cells positioned between the yolk sac and amniotic cavity that will give rise to the embryo.

**Embryonic stage**   Time from the beginning of week three to the end of week eight.

**Endoderm**   The innermost germ layer, which gives rise to the gut, liver, and lungs.

**Endoplasmic reticulum (ER)**   The membranous organelle that is continuous with the nuclear membrane; it is a network of flattened sacs and tubes with some of the membranes studded with ribosomes (rough ER) and some ribosome-free (smooth ER).

**Epiblast**   The cells of the inner cell mass that do not contribute to the hypoblast.

**Epigenesis**   The view of development where structures arise progressively.

**Fertilization**   The fusion of sperm and egg that produces the zygote.

**Fetus**   The developing human from the end of the eighth week until birth.

**Fibroblast**   Connective tissue cell.

**Gamete**   A haploid cell such as a sperm or egg that takes part in sexual reproduction.

**Gastrulation**   Developmental process in which the cells of the embryo undergo significant movements as they rearrange themselves, ultimately leading to the establishment of the three germ layers.

**Gene**    A region of DNA that contains the code for the production of a protein.

**Genome**    The genetic material of an organism, found in the nucleus.

**Genotype**    The genetic makeup of an organism.

**Germ cell**    A differentiated cell that can undergo meiosis to give rise to gametes.

**Germ layers**    The ectoderm, mesoderm, and endoderm, formed by gastrulation during embryonic development; they give rise to all the tissues and organs of the body.

**Golgi apparatus**    An organelle made up of flattened membranous sacs, it stores, modifies, and packages proteins produced in the endoplasmic reticulum. The proteins are eventually delivered to some other location within or outside of the cell.

**Haploid cell**    A cell that contains one set of chromosomes.

***Hox* genes**    A family of genes found in all animals; they are clustered in the genome and are involved in antero-posterior patterning.

**Hypothalamus**    The ventral region of the forebrain that coordinates the endocrine and nervous systems.

**Inner cell mass**    A collection of cells inside the blastocyst that develops into the embryo.

**Mesencephalon**    The midbrain.

**Meiosis**    The type of cell division that occurs only in germ cells; it produces haploid sperm and eggs.

**Mesenchyme**    Connective tissue cells, usually mesoderm, that have the ability to migrate.

**Mesoderm**    The middle germ layer, which gives rise to the skeleton and skeletal muscle.

**Mitochondrion**    Long oval organelles with an outer surrounding membrane and an inner membrane that folds in upon itself; sometimes called the "power plants" of the cell, they are the site of ATP production.

**Mitosis**    Cell division or cellular reproduction, where one cell divides into two virtually identical daughter cells.

**Morphogenesis**    Processes that alter the shape and form of the embryo.

**Morula**    A solid cluster of cells produced by cleavage during the preembryonic stage.

**Neural crest**    A collection of cells that initially links the newly formed neural tube and overlying ectoderm. Neural crest cells migrate extensively throughout the body during development and also give rise to a large number of cell types and structures.

**Neural plate**    The ectodermal cells that are initially induced by the notochord to become neural ectoderm. In response to this induction, the cells that make up the neural plate take on a distinctly elongated and columnar appearance.

**Neural tube**    The embryonic structure that gives rise to the brain and spinal cord and various types of neurons.

**Neurulation**    The developmental process that gives rise to the neural tube.

**Node**    The knotlike structure at the front of the extending primitive streak.

**Notochord**    A transient rodlike structure of cells that runs along the anterior-posterior axis of the embryo and lies beneath the developing central nervous system.

**Nucleotides**. The building blocks of DNA and RNA; nucleotides are made up of a nitrogen-containing base (adenosine, cytosine, guanine, thymine, or uracil), a sugar molecule (deoxyribose or ribose), and a phosphate group.

**Nucleus**    Largest organelle in the cell, it contains the genome.

**Oocyte**    An egg cell.

**Optic vesicle**    Vesicles that develop from the forebrain and give rise to the eyes.

**Organelle**    Cytoplasmic structures that perform specific functions; most are membranous.

**Organogenesis**    Organ development.

**Patterning**    The ordering of cells and structures to produce the general pattern of a structure or of the body itself; the process used to lay down, or map out, the body plan.

**Phenotype**   The appearance of an organism as a result of its genotype.

**Phocomelia**   Birth defect characterized by the child's hands and feet being attached to abbreviated, or shortened, arms and legs.

**Phospholipid**   The major kind of lipid found in biological membranes.

**Placenta**   The structure formed by the chorion that allows the embryo to obtain nutrients and oxygen from the mother while excreting wastes.

**Plasma membrane**   The membrane that surrounds cells and controls the passage of materials into and out of the cell.

**Pluripotent cell**   Cells that have the capacity to form any type of cell or tissue other than those associated with extraembryonic tissues.

**Preembryonic stage**   The first two weeks of human development that precede implantation.

**Primitive groove**   The groove formed when cells move inward and pass through the primitive streak.

**Primitive streak**   A line of cells running along the midline of the embryonic disc during gastrulation.

**Progress zone**   The region of mesenchyme at the distal tip of the developing limb bud.

**Prosencephalon**   The forebrain.

**Proteins**   A class of organic compounds made up of amino acids; each protein is made up of a unique sequence of amino acids.

**Rhombencephalon**   The hindbrain.

**Rhombomere**   A discrete segment that makes up the developing hindbrain.

**Ribonucleic acid**   See RNA.

**Ribosome**   Cell structure made of protein and RNA; involved in translation.

**RNA (ribonucleic acid)**   A nucleic acid that functions in the transcription of DNA and in protein synthesis; made up of adenine, cytosine, guanine, and uracil nucleotides.

**Somatic cell**    Cells, other than germ cells, that make up the body of an organism.

**Somite**    Segmented mesoderm along the anterior-posterior axis of the trunk of the embryo.

**Stylopod**    The most proximal portion of the limbs—the humerus in the arm and the femur in the leg.

**Telencephalon**    The anterior region of the forebrain.

**Teratogen**    Agent that can disrupt development and lead to birth defects.

**Thalamus**    Region of the forebrain that relays sensory information to the cerebrum.

**Transcription**    Copying of the sequence of the coding region of a gene into nucleotide sequence of RNA.

**Translation**    The process in which the information encoded in MRNA is translated into the amino acid sequence of a protein.

**Trophoblast**    The cell layer that makes up the outer sphere of the blastocyst.

**Zeugopod**    The region of the limb adjacent and distal to humerus or femur; contains the ulna and radius in the forearm and the tibia and fibula in the lower leg.

**Zona pellucida**    The protective covering that surrounds the egg.

**Zone of polarizing activity (ZPA)**    A region localized at the posterior margin of the limb bud that acts as a signaling center during limb development.

**Zygote**    The fertilized egg.

# Bibliography

Alberts, B, et al. *Molecular Biology of the Cell,* 4th ed. New York: Garland Science, 2002.

Campbell, K.H., et al. "Sheep Cloned by Nuclear Transfer from a Cultured Cell Line." *Nature.* 380(6569) (1996): 64–66.

Chen, H., et al. "Limb and Kidney Defects in Lmx1b Mutant Mice Suggest an Involvement of LMX1B in Human Nail Patella Syndrome". *Nature Genetics.* 19(1) (1998): 51–55.

Davis, A.P., et al. "Absence of Radius and Ulna in Mice Lacking hoxa-11 and hoxd-11." *Nature.* 375(6534) (1995): 791–5.

Dealy, C.N., et al. "Wnt-5a and Wnt-7a are Expressed in the Developing Chick Limb Bud in a Manner Suggesting Roles in Pattern Formation Along the Proximodistal and Dorsoventral Axes." *Mechanisms of Development.* 43(2-3) (1993): 175–86.

Dreyer, S.D., et al. "Mutations in LMX1B Cause Abnormal Skeletal Patterning and Renal Dysplasia in Nail Patella Syndrome." *Nature Genetics.* 19(1) (1998): 47–50.

Duboule, D. "Making Progress With Limb Models." *Nature.* 418(6897) (2002): 492–493.

Gilbert, S.F. *Developmental Biology,* 8th ed. Sunderland, Mass.: Sinauer Associates, 2006.

Johnson, M.D. *Human Biology Concepts and Current Issues* Second Edition. San Francisco: Benjamin Cummings, 2003.

Kalthoff, K. *Analysis of Biological Development,* 2nd Edition. New York: McGraw Hill, 2001.

Knightley, P., H. Evans, E. Potter, and M. Wallace. *Suffer the Children: The Story of Thalidomide.* New York: Viking Press, 1979.

Le Mouellic, H., et al. "Homeosis in the Mouse Induced by a Null Mutation in the Hox-3.1 Gene." *Cell.* 69(2) (1992): 251–264.

Muragaki, Y., et al. "Altered Growth and Branching Patterns in Synpolydactyly Caused by Mutations in HOXD13." *Science.* 272(5261) (1996): 548–551.

Parr, B.A., et al. "Mouse Wnt Genes Exhibit Discrete Domains of Expression in the Early Embryonic CNS and Limb Buds." *Development.* 119(1) (1993): 247–261.

Prentice, D.A. *Stem Cells and Cloning.* San Francisco: Benjamin Cummings, 2003.

Riddle, R.D., et al. "Sonic Hedgehog Mediates the Polarizing Activity of the ZPA." *Cell.* 75(7) (1993): 1401–1416.

Riddle, R.D. and C. Tabin. "How Limbs Develop." *Scientific American.* 280(2) (1999): 74–79.

Saunders, J.W.J. "The Proximo-distal Sequence of Origin of the Parts of the Chick Wing and the Role of the Ectoderm." *Journal of Experimental Zoology.* 108 (1948): 363–403.

Stephens, T.D. *Dark Remedy: The Impact of Thalidomide and its Revival as a Vital Medicine.* Cambridge, Mass.: Perseus Publishers, 2001.

Sulik, K., et al. "Morphogenesis of the Murine Dode and Notochordal Plate." *Developmental Dynamics.* 201(3) (1994): 260–278.

Thorogood, P. *Embryos, Genes, and Birth Defects.* Chichester, N.Y.: J. Wiley, 1997.

Ulijaszek, S.J., et al. *The Cambridge Encyclopedia of Human Growth and Development.* Cambridge, U.K.; New York, N.Y.: Cambridge University Press, 1998.

Vieille-Grosjean, I., et al. "Branchial HOX Gene Expression and Human Craniofacial Development." *Dev Biol.* 183(1) (1997): 49–60.

Wolpert, L. *The Triumph of the Embryo.* Oxford: Oxford University Press, 1991.

Wolpert, L. *Principles of Development.* 3rd ed. Oxford: Oxford University Press, 2007.

Yonei-Tamura, S., et al. "FGF7 and FGF10 Directly Induce the Apical Ectodermal Ridge in Chick Embryos." *Developmental Biology.* 211(1) (1999): 133–143.

# Further Resources

Nüsslein-Volhard, C. *Coming to Life: How Genes Drive Development.* Carlsbad, CA: Kales Press, 2006.

*Nature* Special Issue. "The Human Genome." Vol. 409 (Feb. 15, 2001). 745–964.

*Science* Special Issue. "Stem Cell Research and Ethics." Vol. 287, 5457 (Feb. 25, 2000). 1353–1544.

*Science* Special Issue. "The Human Genome." Vol. 291, 5507 (Feb. 16, 2001). 1145–1434.

Nova Special: "Life's Greatest Miracle." Originally broadcast November 20, 2001 (also see http://www.pbs.org/wgbh/nova/miracle/).

## Web sites

### Illinois Teratogen Information Service
Information on teratogens and human development
*http://www.fetal-exposure.org/*

### KidsHealth
Information about development as well as early childhood health and behavior
*http://www.kidshealth.org/index.html*

### March of Dimes
A non-profit organization dedicated to preventing birth defects
*http://www.marchofdimes.com*

### Medline Plus, part of the U.S. National Institutes of Health and the National Library of Medicine
Information on Birth Defects
*http://www.nlm.nih.gov/medlineplus/birthdefects.html*

**Society for Developmental Biology**
An international society dedicated to furthering the study of embryological development of all organisms
*http://www.sdbonline.org/*

**The Virtual Embryo**
Interactive information about developmental biology
*http://www.ucalgary.ca/UofC/eduweb/virtualembryo/*

**Virtual Library of Developmental Biology by Scott Gilbert (author of *Developmental Biology*)**
Includes links to research and journal articles about organisms, genomes, and related topics.
*http://www.sdbonline.org/index.php?option=content&task=view&id=23*

**Westside Pregnancy Clinic**
Web site details the stages of fetal development
*http://www.w-cpc.org/fetal.html*

# Picture Credits

# Index

# About the Author

Ted Zerucha, Ph.D., was educated at the University of Manitoba in Winnipeg, Canada, and at the University of Ottawa in Ottawa, Canada. He received his Bachelor of Science Honors degree from the Department of Biochemistry and Masters of Science degree from the Department of Microbiology, both at the University of Manitoba. He earned his Ph.D. in 1999 from the Department of Cellular and Molecular Medicine/Anatomy and Neurobiology at the University of Ottawa, where he studied at the Loeb Health Research Institute of the Ottawa Hospital. He has also held research positions at the University of Chicago and at Argonne National Laboratory. He is now a member of the faculty of the Department of Biology at Appalachian State University, where he teaches courses based on his primary research interests, developmental and evolutionary biology and cellular and molecular biology. Zerucha has published a number of research papers, including articles in the *Journal of Neuroscience, Mechanisms of Development, Biochemistry and Cell Biology,* and *Nucleic Acids Research.* He has also had his work presented at a large number of conferences across North America and Europe.